Bitcoin Programming

Mostafa Farghaly

Table of Contents

Chapter 1: Bitcoin Server

The Bitcoin Core client from bitcoin.org comes in two flavors, one with a graphical user interface named bitcoin-qt which acts as a full fledged Bitcoin wallet, and the other is a headless command-line program named bitcoind "bitcoin daemon". They are completely compatible with each other, take the same command-line arguments, read the same configuration files, and write the same data files. You can launch them as a JSON-RPC server and interact with them through command-line or through JSON-RPC library of your favorite programming language as we will see in <u>Chapter 2: JSON-RPC</u>.

bitcoin**d** is functioning as both client and a server, you can start it as a server as we will see in the next sections, and you can use it as a client to tell the running server what to do.

Bitcoin Core client version 0.9.0 introduced bitcoin-cli as JSON-RPC client-only, where the client functionality of bitcoind will be removed in the upcoming releases, so it's recommended to use bitcoind as server-only and use the newly introduced bitcoin-cli as a client.

Program	function
Bitcoin-qt	Server and client through console window
Bitcoind	Client and server
Bitcoin-cli	Client-only

Installing Bitcoin Core

You can download Bitcoin Core client from https://bitcoin.org/en/download .
You'll finds Windows installers and Mac disk images which are few clicks
away to install. If you're Linux user, you'll find both 32-bit and 64-bit
executables, and Bitcoin Core client source code, if you want to build it. If
you're Ubuntu user, Bitcoin has officially maintained ppa at
https://launchpad.net/~bitcoin/+archive/bitcoin add this ppa to your
system's software sources:

```
sudo add-apt-repository ppa:bitcoin/bitcoin
sudo apt-get update
```

If you don't have add-apt-repository binary, type the following, then run the
previous commands again:

```
sudo apt-get install python-software-properties
```

then install bitcoin-qt:

```
sudo apt-get install bitcoin-qt
```

install bitcoind and bitcoin-cli:

```
sudo apt-get install bitcoind
```

Happy hacking :)

From now till the end of the book, i will assume that all executable
programs are in your PATH, including bitcoin-qt, bitcoind, and bitcoin-cli.
Add them if they're not already in your PATH.

Hello Bitcoin

Let's run Bitcoin as a server, simply open a terminal window and type:

```
bitcoin-qt -server
```

and you'll get the error message shown in the next picture:

or in case of bitcoind type:

```
bitcoind -daemon
```

you'll get the same error message !

Both error messages inform you that you can't run Bitcoin Core client as a server without setting `rpcuser` and `rpcpassword` in the configuration file, and recommend you to use `alertnotify` to be notified of possible problems. What ?

`rpcuser` is the username for the JSON-RPC connection, and `rpcpassword` is the password of the JSON-RPC connection. Configuration file is a file named bitcoin.conf contains a list of key=value pairs, one per line, with optional comments starting with # character, located in the data directory. We will discuss alertnotify in Chapter 6: Notifications.

Data Directory

In windows goto data directory by opening run window by Windows+R and type

```
%APPDATA%/bitcoin
```

It'll open `C:\Documents and Settings\username\Application Data\Bitcoin` in windows XP, and `C:\Users\username\AppData\Roaming\Bitcoin` in windows Vista, 7, and 8.

In Linux data directory is `~/.bitcoin`

Note that directories starting with dot "." are hidden in Linux, you need to:

```
ls -a
```

to show them.

In Mac data directory is ~/library/ApplicationSupport/Bitcoin

Configuring Bitcoin Server

Create bitcoin.conf file in the data directory, and add the following lines to it:

```
rpcuser=bitcoinrpc
rpcpassword=p0ssw0rd
```

Save the file and open new terminal window and type the following:

```
bitcoin-qt -server
```

If everything is fine, bitcoin-qt will open without any error messages, open a new terminal and type:

```
bitcoin-cli getinfo
```

and you'll get response like this:

```
{
    "version" : 90100,
    "protocolversion" : 70002,
    "walletversion" : 60000,
    "balance" : 0.11990000,
    "blocks" : 256214,
    "timeoffset" : 0,
    "connections" : 8,
```

```
        "proxy" : "",
        "difficulty" : 1088.10584687,
        "testnet" : true,
        "keypoololdest" : 1400704976,
        "keypoolsize" : 101,
        "paytxfee" : 0.00000000,
        "errors" : ""
    }
```

or type

```
    bitcoin-cli help
```

and you'll get an overview of all available RPC commands.
In case of bitcoind, type:

```
    bitcoind -daemon
```

within a minute you'll get this response:

```
    bitcoin server starting
```

If bitcoind doesn't respond don't worry, don't close the terminal window and open a new terminal window and call the getinfo method

```
    bitcoin-cli getinfo
```

and you'll get response like the getinfo's response above.
Bitcoin server works fine. What to do next ? Daydream, you'll be rich and

famous.

Stopping the Server

You can stop the running bitcoin server by calling "stop" command:

```
bitcoin-cli stop
```

stop command will shutdown bitcoin-qt and will kill running bitcoind thread.

Configuration File VS. Command line arguments

All command-line arguments may be specified in configuration file and vise versa, except -datadir and -conf are command-line arguments only. -datadir specify the data directory, and -conf specify the configuration file. For a full list of command line arguments and configuration file options goto Appendix A

For example if you want to change your data directory to c:/ and your configuration file to coco.conf, start bitcoin-qt like this

```
bitcoin-qt -datadir=c:/ -conf=coco.conf
```

Configuration file is more convenient than command-line arguments, where you type the key=value settings once in bitcoin.conf and it will take effect every time you open bitcoin-qt or bitcoind. For example if you want to open bitcoin every time as a server, you can either add this line to bitcoin.conf **once**:

```
server=1
```

or open a new terminal run bitcoin-qt or bitcoind with -server argument
every time.

Chapter 2: JSON-RPC

JSON-RPC is lightweight remote procedure call protocol similar to XML-RPC. It's designed to be simple. The general mechanism consists of two peers establishing a data connection. During the lifetime of a connection, peers may invoke methods provided by the other peer. To invoke a remote method, a request object serialized as JSON is sent. Unless the request is a notification it must be replied to with a response object serialized as JSON.

A remote method is invoked by sending a request to a remote service using HTTP or a TCP/IP socket (starting with version 2.0). When using HTTP, the content-type may be defined as application/json.

All transfer types are a single object, serialized using JSON. A request object is a call to a specific method provided by a remote system. It must contain these three properties:

- **method** - A String with the name of the method to be invoked.

- **params** - An Array of objects to be passed as parameters to the defined method.

- **id** - A value of any type, which is used to match the response with the request that it is replying to.

The receiver of the request must reply with a valid response object to all received requests. The response must contain these three properties:

1) **result** - The data returned by the invoked method. If an error occurred while invoking the method, this value must be null.

2) **error** - A specified Error code if there was an error invoking the

method, otherwise null.

3) **id** - The id of the request it is responding to.

Since there are situations where no response is needed or even desired, notifications were introduced. A notification is similar to a request except for the id, which is not needed because no response will be returned. In this case the id property should be omitted (Version 2.0) or be null (Version 1.0).

Here's an example of requests starting with → and responses starting with ← :

```
→ {"methdod": "sum", "params": [1,2], "id": 0}
← {"result": 3, "error": null, "id": 0}


→  {"method": "getbalance", "params": [], "id": 1}
←  {"result": 79.50000000, "error": null, "id": 1}


→  {"method": "getnewaddress", "params": [], "id": 2}
←  {"result": "mfxyDWEtjcuEPkNXGADaick4DiWbsiTENx",
"error": null, "id": 2}
```

Proper Money Handling

Bitcoin Core client store all balances and transaction values as 64-bit integers, where 1 btc = 100,000,000 satoshi (One hundred million of the smallest possible bitcoin value, named after Satoshi Nakamoto the pseudonym of the inventor of Bitcoin). On the other hand in JSON-RPC API values are expressed as double precision numbers, where 1 btc is expressed as 1.00000000

Bitcoin Core Client	JSON-RPC

100,000,000 satoshi	1.00000000 btc
195,000,000 satoshi	1.95000000 btc
5,500,000,000 satoshi	55.00000000 btc
78,412,546,600 satoshi	784.12546600 btc

You can implement this conversion in python like this:

```
def amountToJSON(value):
    return float(value / 1e8)

def JSONToAmount(value):
    return long(value * 1e8)
```

The general rule to convert from double to 64-bit intger is to multiply by 100,000,000 and round to the nearest integer, and to convert from 64-bit integer to double is to divide by 100,000,000.0 and make sure that the result has 8 or more digits after the decimal point including padding zeros.

JSON-RPC Libraries

This section is an overview of JSON-RPC libraries implemented in 4 different programming languages: Python, PHP, Ruby, and JavaScript. why ? because i believe they're the most used programming languages for developing web services. For each programming languages you will found at least one implementation, i don't recommend anyone of them, choose the one that best suits your project's needs, you may end up implementing your own library. For a complete list of JSON-RPC libraries check JSON-RPC wikipedia page http://en.wikipedia.org/wiki/JSON-RPC#Implementations or search your programming language repository or package manager.

Python

I will cover bitcoinrpc library by Jeff Garzik, you can download it from https://github.com/jgarzik/python-bitcoinrpc . Bitcoinrpc library is a fork of jsonrpc library http://json-rpc.org/wiki/python-json-rpc . It includes the following improvements over jsonrpc library:

- HTTP connections persists for the life of the AuthServiceProxy object

- Sends JSON-RPC "version" parameter

- Uses standard python JSON library

Bitcoinrpc library is very simple that it consists of two classes: AuthServiceProxy and JSONRPCException. Import both classes:

```
from bitcoinrpc.authproxy import AuthServiceProxy,
JSONRPCException
```

AuthServiceProxy class is used to obtain new persistent connection to the Bitcoin JSON RPC server

```
bitcoin =
AuthServiceProxy("http://rpcuser:rpcpassssword@host:port")
```

replace rpcuser and rpcpassword with the settings in your bitcoin.conf file, replace host with 127.0.0.1 in case of local host, replace port with 8332 in case of mainnet, and 18332 in case of testnet or regtest. We will use testnet till the end of the book, for more information on testnet Chpater 3: Testing.

```
    rpcuser = "bitcoinrpc"
    rpcpassword = "p0ssw0rd"
    host = "127.0.0.1"
    port = "18332"
    bitcoin = AuthServiceProxy("http://" + rpcuser + ":" +
rpcpassword + "@" + host + ":"  + port)
```

JSONRPCException is the exception raised when something goes wrong:

```
    try:
        print bitcoin.getinfo()
        print bitcoin.getnewaddress()
        address = "mimoZNLcP2rrMRgdeX5PSnR7AjCqQveZZ4"
        print bitcoin.sendtoaddress(address, 25)
    except JSONRPCException as e:
        print e.error
```

Check the error's code to take the appropriate action

```
    except JSONRPCException as e:
        if e.error["code"] == -5:
            # Invalid bitcoin address, do something
```

Ruby

rpcjson library is a modern Ruby implementation of JSON-RPC standards 1.1 and 2.0, developed by Jonathan Jeffus, you can download its source code from https://github.com/jjeffus/rpcjson you can install it using gem:

```
    gem install rpcjson
```

then require it in your project:

```
require "rpcjson"
```

create a new JSON-RPC Client using RPC::JSON::Client class:

```ruby
server_addr = "http://rpcuser:rpcpass@ip:port"
# 1.1 is Bitcoin JSON-RPC protocol version
# default value is 2.0
bitcoin = RPC::JSON::Client.new server_addr, 1.1
info = bitcoin.getinfo
info.each do |k,v|
    puts k, "=>", v
end
```

RPC::JSON::Client::Error will be raised if something goes wrong:

```ruby
begin
    addr = bitcoin.getnewaddress
    bitcoin.validateaddress addr
    bitcoin.sendtoaddress addr, 999.99
rescue RPC::JSON::Client.Error => e
    puts e.error["code"]
    puts e.error["message"]
end
```

JavaScript

Node-Bitcoin by Sean Lavine https://github.com/freewil/node-bitcoin is a simple wrapper for the Bitcoin Core client's JSON-RPC API , install it using node package manager:

```
npm install bitcoin
```

after it's successfully installed, open node REPL in your command-line:

```
node
```

then require it:

```
var bitcoin = require("bitcoin")
```

create a new bitcoin.Client object:

```
var client = new bitcoin.Client({
    user: "rpcuser",
    pass: "rpcpass",
    host: "127.0.0.1",
    port: "18332"
});
```

Bitcoin RPC API is exposed as lower camel case methods on the bitcoin.Client object, for example you can call getinfo method as:

```
client.getInfo(function(error, info){
    console.log(error ? error : info);
});
```

At the time of writing this paragraph, node-bitcoin doesn't support all Bitcoin RPC methods ! It's supporting methods up to Bitcoin 0.8.0, however this isn't a problem. Node-bitcoin has a method called cmd on the bitcoin.Client object, you can use it to call any RPC method:

```
// getunconfirmedbalance is supported by Bitcoin Core 0.9.0+
// not exposed as bitcon.Client method
client.cmd("getunconfirmedbalance", function(error, balance){
      if(error){
            console.log(error.code);
            console.log(error.message);
      } else {
            console.log(balance);
      }
});
```

Another interesting Bitcoin libary to check out is Bitcore library from Bitpay company http://bitcore.io.

PHP

JSON-RPC-PHP is a JSON-RPC server and client implemented in PHP, you can download it here http://jsonrpcphp.org . Require it in your PHP project and create a new jsonRPCClient object:

```
require("jsonRPCClient.php");
$bitcoin = new jsonRPCClient(http://user:pass@host:port);
$info = $bitcoin->getinfo();
print $info["version"];
print $bitcoin->getbalance();
print $bitcoin->getnewaddress();
```

jsonRPCClient.php uses fopen() function, and if something goes wrong like calling deprecated method, or method with wrong type or number of arguments, you'll get an Exception with message "Unable to connect to ..." if it received 404 or 500 HTTP errors, this will prevent you from seeing the error messages returned by the Bitcoin server, because they're sent with HTTP status 404 or 500.

EasyBitcoin-PHP is a simple class for making calls to Bitcoin API using PHP developed by Andrew LeCody, it doesn't have issue with responses with 404 or 500 status, you can download it here https://github.com/aceat64/EasyBitcoin-PHP it uses cURL so you must install it and configure it to work with PHP http://php.net/manual/en/book.curl.php. Here's a simple example:

```
require("easybitcoin.php");
$bitcoin = new Bitcoin("user", "pass", "127.0.0.1",
"18332");
print $bitcoin->getbalance();
$info = $bitcoin->getinfo();
print $info["version"];
```

When a call fails for any reason, it will return false and put the error message in $bitcoin->error:

```
if($bitcoin->makemehappy()){
    print "I am Happy :)";
} else {
    print $error->message;
}
```

HTTP status code can be found in $bitcoin->status, full response is stored in $bitcoin->response, and raw JSON response is stored in $bitcoin->raw_response.

Another interesting PHP JSON-RPC library to checkout is Tivoka

Getting Help

If you want to list all JSON-RPC commands supported by Bitcoin Server, or get help for specific command, Bitcoin Core has JSON-RPC help method:

```
help <command>
```

where, <command> is the command -method- name you want to get help for, if you omit <command> it will list all commands supported by the running Bitcoin Core. You can call it from Bitcoin-qt RPC console, from "help" menu > debug window, then open console tab:

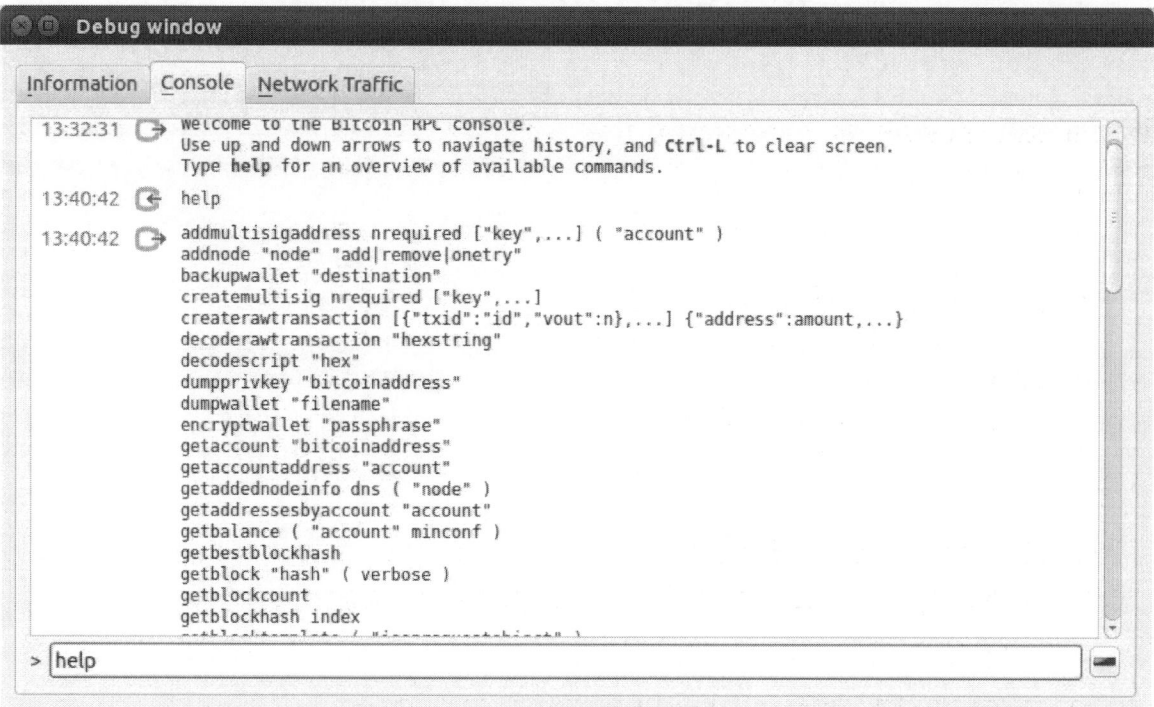

or from bitcoin-cli:

```
farghaly@farghaly: ~
farghaly@farghaly:~$ bitcoin-cli help getnewaddress
getnewaddress ( "account" )

Returns a new Bitcoin address for receiving payments.
If 'account' is specified (recommended), it is added to the address book
so payments received with the address will be credited to 'account'.

Arguments:
1. "account"        (string, optional) The account name for the address to be li
nked to. if not provided, the default account "" is used. It can also be set to
the empty string "" to represent the default account. The account does not need
to exist, it will be created if there is no account by the given name.

Result:
"bitcoinaddress"    (string) The new bitcoin address

Examples:
> bitcoin-cli getnewaddress
> bitcoin-cli getnewaddress ""
> bitcoin-cli getnewaddress "myaccount"
> curl --user myusername --data-binary '{"jsonrpc": "1.0", "id":"curltest", "met
hod": "getnewaddress", "params": ["myaccount"] }' -H 'content-type: text/plain;'
 http://127.0.0.1:8332/
```

Error codes

When something goes wrong, Bitcoin server will reply with response object where "result" property is null and "error" is not null this time:

```
{
        id=
        result=null
        error={
                mesage=
```

```
            code=
      }
  }
```

in this response, "error" object contains two properties: message is text explaining why the error happened, code is negative number specific to each error. All error codes can be found in rpcprotocol.h file in Bitcoin Core client source code at github. Appendix B contains a summary of error codes, check it out.

Chapter 3: Testing

Testnet

Testnet is an alternate blockchain used mainly for developing and testing bitcoin applications without using real bitcoins and without touching the main bitcoin blockchain on the mainnet. You can obtain Testnet coins online for free as we'll see in the next sections or you can mine them. Testnet bitcoins are useless, so don't trade them or buy anything with them. Testnet genesis block may be reset anytime and if that happened you'll lose all your testnet coins. At the time of writing this book we're on Testnet 3.

Start bitcoin-qt or bitcoind with -testnet argument:

```
bitcoin-qt -testnet
bitcoind -testnet
```

or add

```
testnet=1
```

to the configuration file if you want to be on testnet every time you use Bitcoin Core client.

After starting bitcoin-qt you'll see the splash screen with large green bitcoin logo instead of the orange one.

If you're running bitcoind, call getinfo and you'll see the testnet flag:

```
bitcoin-cli getinfo
```

will return something like this:

```
{
        "version" : 90100,
        "protocolversion" : 70002,
        "walletversion" : 60000,
        "balance" : 0.11990000,
        "blocks" : 256257,
        "timeoffset" : 0,
        "connections" : 0,
        "proxy" : "",
        "difficulty" : 1088.10584687,
        "testnet" : true,
        "keypoololdest" : 1400704976,
        "keypoolsize" : 101,
        "paytxfee" : 0.00000000,
        "errors" : ""
}
```

Testnet differs from the mainnet in that:

- Testnet JSON-RPC connection port is 18332, mainnet is 8332.

- Testnet Bitcoin network protocol listens to port 18333, mainnet is 8333.

- Testnet addresses has version byte 0x6f, mainnet is 0x00.

- Testnet addresses usually start with m or n.

- Testnet has minimum mining difficulty of 1.0.

- Testnet has a different genesis block, you can find it here http://blockexplorer.com/testnet/b/0

- The isStandard() check is disabled, so you can experiment with non standard transactions like funding/spending multi-signatures addresses, replacement transaction , contracts … etc.

Obtaining Testnet bitcoins

Testnet bitcoins are available online for free from online faucets like TP's Testnet Faucet http://tpfaucet.appspot.com/ . If you want to get some, start bitcoin-qt on Testnet, goto "receive" tab if you're using Bitcoin Core client up to version 0.8.6 , or if you're using Bitcoin Core client 0.9+ from File menu > "Receiving addresses", create new address from "+ new address" button and give it a label like "TP Faucet". Wait for the client to synchronize with the network, open the TP's Testnet Faucet website, paste your testnet bitcoin address in the website, write the captcha and press send. At the time of writing the book the website sends 9.5 bitcoins per request. When you're done with developing and testing your kickass Bitcoin application send your Testnet bitcoins back to the address in the website.

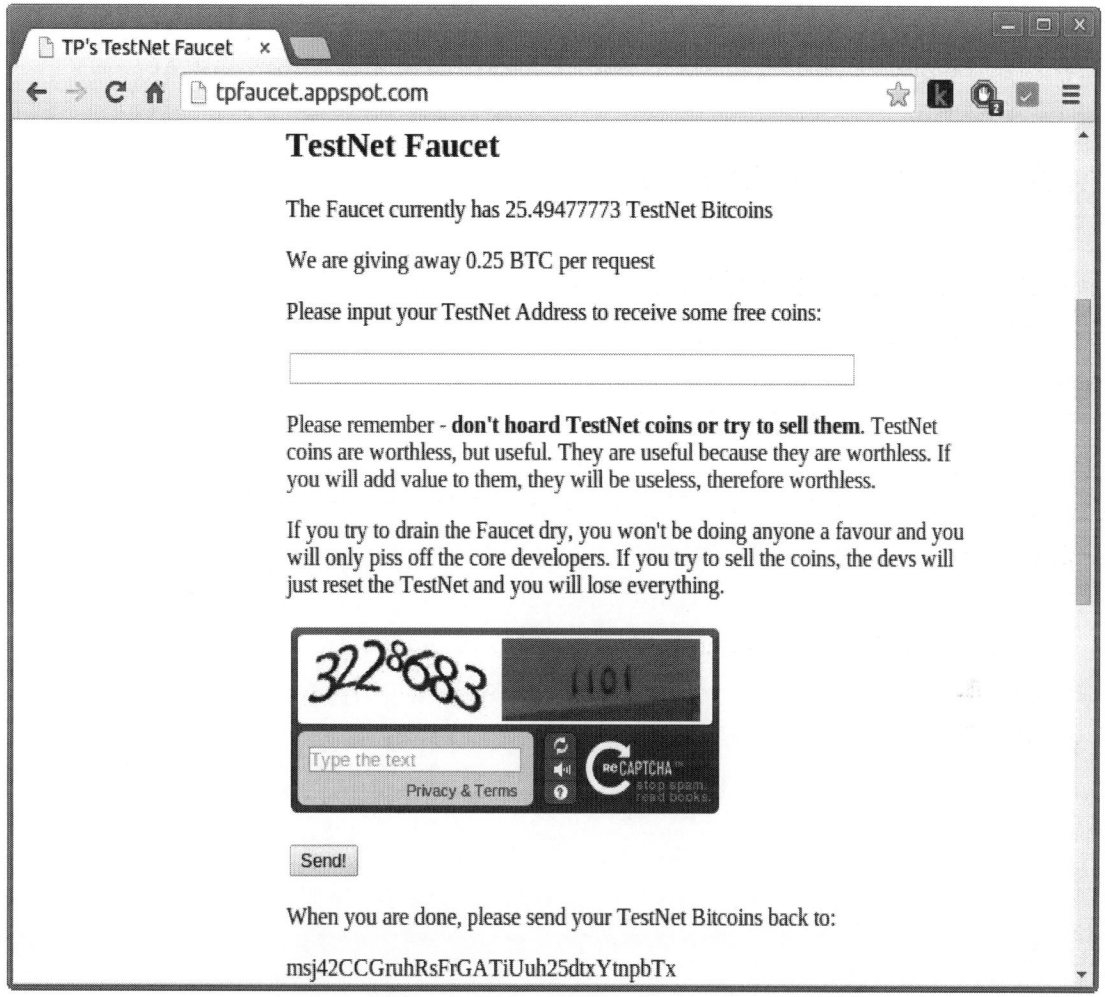

Another interesting testnet Faucet is http://faucet.xeno-genesis.com check it out.

Mining on Testnet

Start bitcoind on testnet:

```
bitcoind -testnet -printtoconsole
```

-printtoconsole will send tarce and debug info to the console instead of debug.log file. Verify mining by calling gethashespersec method which will return your hashing power:

```
bitcoin-cli gethashespersec
```

to get the difficulty of testnet:

```
bitcoin-cli getdifficulty
```

difficulty on testnet is increasing because testers use GPU and ASICS to mine on testnet, it'll take a long time before your first bitcoins are generated, and generated coins will mature after 120 blocks ! In Bitcoin 0.9 generated coins mature at 101 blocks, so mining on testnet isn't practical.

Regtest

Bitcoin Core client version 0.9 introduced -regtest mode, which is similar to testnet, but private with difficulty=0 and instant block generation.

Start bitcoin-qt or bitcoind with -regtest option:

```
bitcoin-qt -regtest
```

if your bitcoin.conf file contains testnet=1, you'll be alerted of invalid combination of -regtest and -testnet:

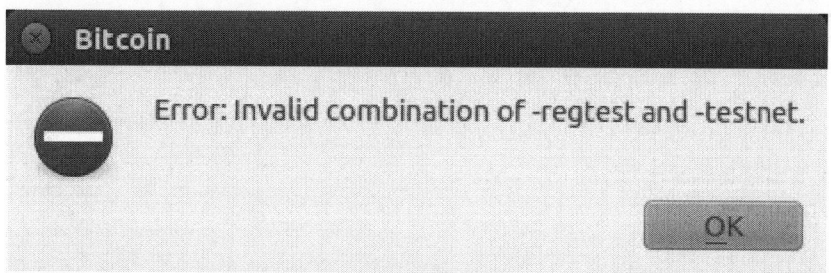

remove testnet=1 from your bitcoin.conf file, or start bitcoin with -notestnet option:

```
bitcoin-qt -regtest -notestnet
```

Bitcoin-qt will start with private testnet (regtest) mode, you can generate new blocks any time you want and get 50 bitcoins as a block reward by calling setgenerate method:

```
bitcoin-cli setgenerate true
```

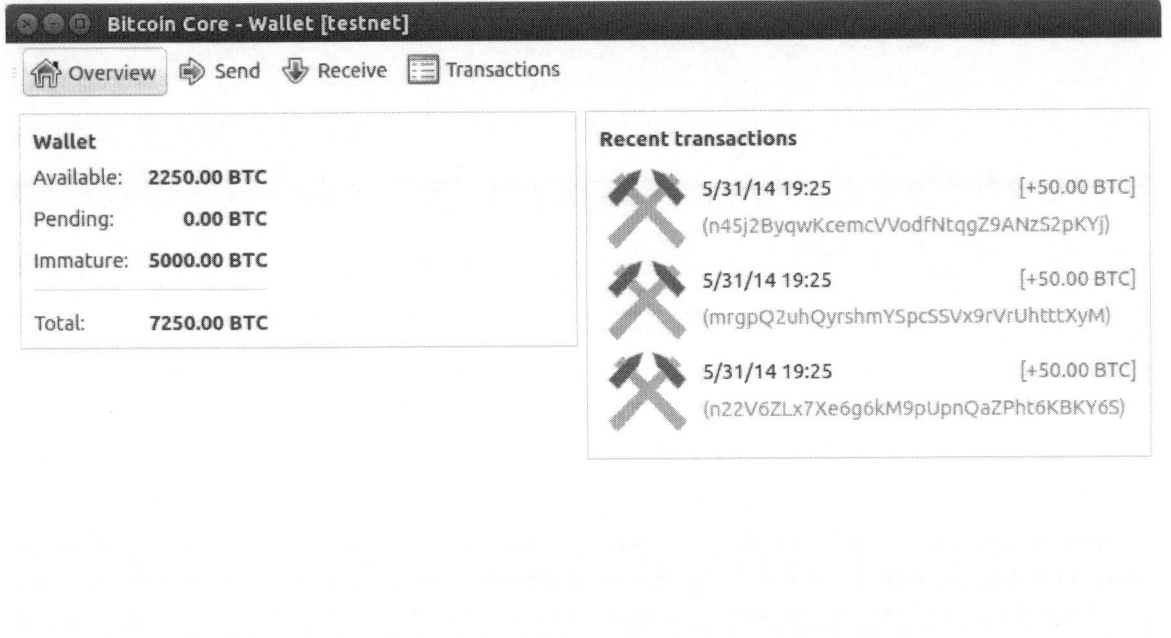

Generated coins will mature after 101 blocks, so if you want to obtain 50 * n **mature** bitcoins , generate (n+100) blocks. Fortunately, in -regtest mode, the second argument to setgenerate method controls how many blocks are generated immediately, to generate 1500 mature bitcoins:

```
bitcoin-cli setgenerate true 130
```

130 blocks will generate (130-100) * 50 = 1500 mature bitcoins.

Chapter 4: Accounts and Addresses

Bitcoin Core client has an interesting feature called "accounts", which you can use to group receiving addresses under different account names, and you can use it in your Bitcoin application to give each user an account, when an address receives some bitcoins in a transaction, funds (transaction output) will be associated with this address, and the balance of the account associated with this address will be increase accordingly. When you send bitcoins from an account using RPC method like sendfrom as we will see in Chapter 5: Transactions, Bitcoin Core client will select funds associated with its addresses, and account's balance will be decreased accordingly. Think of it as a tree structure where Bitcoin Core client has several accounts, and each account has different addresses, and each address has funds from different transactions. Wallet > account > address > fund (transaction output).

Note that information about accounts are not transmitted to the Bitcoin network, and aren't recorded in the block chain.

Default Account

Bitcoin comes with a default account called "" empty JSON string. Generated coins of solo mining are credited to the default account, and sentoaddress method debits from the default account as we will see in the discussion of sendtoaddress method in Chapter 5: Transactions. In bitcoin-qt default account's addresses has no label, as indicated with (no label) in the next picture:

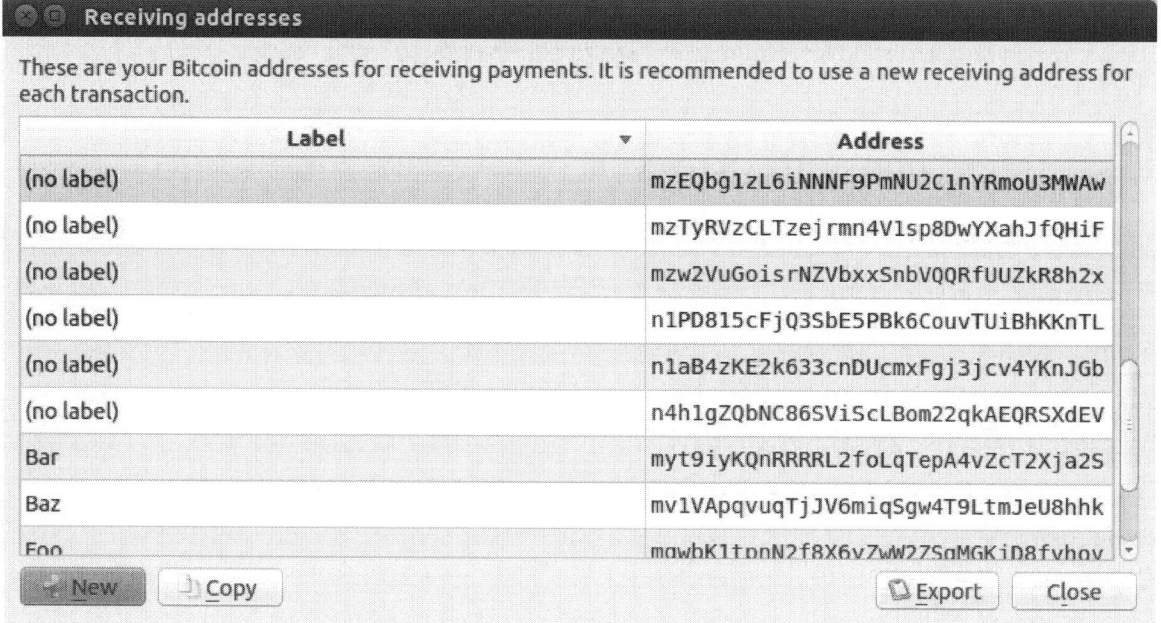

Creating New Account

You can create a new account or check the address of an existing account using getaccountaddress method, which takes one argument <account> the name of the account.

```
getaccountaddress <account>
```

If you give getaccountaddress method a name of an account that doesn't previously exist it will create new account and associate a new receiving address to this account. If you want to check the address of the default account:

```
bitcoin-cli getaccountaddress ""
```

if you want to create a new account:

```
bitcoin-cli getaccountaddress "farghaly"
```

this will create a new account called "farghaly" if it doesn't exist, and will create a new receiving address, and will associate this address to the new account, so any bitcoins sent to this address will be credited "farghaly" account.

Account names are case-sensitive and can be any string except "*" because it's used as wildcard instead of account name as we will see later in the discussion of getbalance method. If you tried to create account with name "*":

```
bitcoin-cli getaccountaddress "*"
```

you'll get "Invalid account name" error with code -11.

The next two method calls will generate two receiving addresses and associate them with two different accounts due to account name case-sensitivity:

```
bitcoin-cli getaccountaddress foo
bitcoin-cli getaccountaddress FOO
```

getaccountaddress method will return the same address until bitcoins are received on that address, it will generate and return new address. why ? to improve your anonymity and make it a bit difficult for other people to track how many bitcoins you have and where you're spending them. Here's how it works

```
bitcoin-cli getaccountaddress foo → D1
```

```
bitcoin-cli getaccountaddress foo → D1
someone sent 5 bitcoins to address D1
bitcoin-cli getaccountaddress foo → D2
```

This doesn't mean that addresses D1 will become useless afterwards. This address will work as long as bitcoin network is up and running.

This method comes in handy in services like online wallet, where you display to each user in his profile page his main bitcoin address, like www.blockchain.info my wallet page as shown in this figure. When someone send you bitcoins to this address it'll change automatically the next time the site call getaccountaddress method.

This Is Your Bitcoin Address
194wdKc1spbCk8h4BmiyESzGo3xGQ6nbnR
Share this with anyone and they can send you payments.

Technical Details of Bitcoin Address

Bitcoin uses Elliptic Curve Digital Signature Algorithm "ECDSA" to generate private and public keys, and to sign transaction and verify signatures. Private key is a random 256-bit number. Public key is 512-bit number calculated from the private key, but the private key can't be calculated from the public key. Bitcoin address is a 160-bit hash of the public key. Address can't be calculated from public key. Private key is used to sign transactions spending funds received on an address and is kept secret in your wallet.dat file, if you lose it, funds received on its address are lost forever. Anyone who knows your public key can verify that the signature is valid and you're the owner of bitcoins in these transactions and hence valid.

Private key → public key → address.

Here are the steps to create a Bitcoin address, in <u>Chapter 7: Keys</u> we will implement this steps in Python:

- Given a random private key

18E14A7B6A307F426A94F8114701E7C8E774E7F9A47E2C2035DB29A206321725

- Take the corresponding public key derived from it

0450863AD64A87AE8A2FE83C1AF1A8403CB53F53E486D8511DAD8A04887E5B23
522CD470243453A299FA9E77237716103ABC11A1DF38855ED6F2EE187E9C582B
A6

- Perform SHA-256 on (2)

600FFE422B4E00731A59557A5CCA46CC183944191006324A447BDB2D98D4B408

- Perform RIPEMD-160 on (3)

010966776006953D5567439E5E39F86A0D273BEE

- Add network version bytes in front of (4), network bytes is **0x00** for mainnet and **0x6f** for testnet3

00010966776006953D5567439E5E39F86A0D273BEE

- Perform SHA-256 on (5)

445C7A8007A93D8733188288BB320A8FE2DEBD2AE1B47F0F50BC10BAE845C094

- Perform SHA-256 again but this time on (6)

D61967F63C7DD183914A4AE452C9F6AD5D462CE3D277798075B107615C1A8A30

- Take the first four bytes of (7), this is the address checksum. Checksum is used for address validation and detecting errors. as we'll see in Chapter 7: Keys

D61967F6

- Add this checksum to the end of (5)

00010966776006953D5567439E5E39F86A0D273BEE**D61967F6**

- Perform Base58Check on (9)

16UwLL9Risc3QfPqBUvKofHmBQ7wMtjvM

Congratulations, now you have a valid *mainnet* bitcoin address, you can import its private key to your bitcoin client using importprivkey method and use it right away. But if you tried to import our address's ECDSA private key using importprivkey method you'll get "Invalid private key" error with code -5, why ? because importprivatekey need another format of the private key called WIF "wallet import format", for more information on how to get the

WIF from ECDSA format, goto <u>Chapter 7: Keys</u>.

Note that Base58Check in setp (10) is a variant of the base58 encoding to eliminate visual ambiguity of similarly looking characters in some fonts like zero 0 and uppercase o "O", lowercase L "l" and Uppercase i "I".

Creating New Addresses

Bitcoin addresses are free, you can generate tens of thousands of them at no cost, you can generate these addresses offline ! with a probability that two users generate the same address of 1 in 2^160, this is like searching for an atom in our expanding universe, Bitcoin address space contains about 1,460,000,000,000,000,000,000,000,000,000,000,000,000,000,000,000 addresses ! If bitcoin address collision happened, users who have the private key of the address can spend funds received on this address if any, there're chances that this address is abandoned or has zero funds.

Use getnewaddress method to generate new address, which takes one optional argument [account] the name of the account to associate the new address to

```
getnewaddress [account]
```

If you omit [account] the generated address will be associated to the default account "".

```
bitcoin-cli getnewaddress "farghaly"
```

will generate a new address and associate it to the account named "farghaly".

```
Bitcoin-cli getnewaddress
```

will generate a new address and associate it to the default account "".

Generating new address for account named "*":

```
bitcoin-cli getnewaddress "*"
```

will return "Invalid account name" error with code -5.

You should give your application's users the ability to create new addresses and labeling them for different uses so they can remember what they're intended to be used for, for example on blockchain.info wallet i've created an address for cloud mining, another address for this book for receiving tips … etc. Labeling addresses isn't a bitcoin feature, implement it yourself.

Address's Public key

If you want to get the public key of an address, use validateaddress method to make sure that the address is valid. If the address is valid, this method will return an object with pubkey property containing the public key:

```
validateaddress <address>
```

Here's an example:

```python
# python
address = "mvCVuo5KcbuSWRCXgcFcnZAyKotoyoFbEw"
res = bitcoin.validateaddress(address)
valid = res["isvalid"]
if valid:
```

```
print res["pubkey"]
```

this method will return pubkey if the address is valid and in your local wallet.dat file, you can't use it to get the public key of foreign address. Public key can't be calculated form address because address is a 160-bit hash of the public key, validateaddress simply fetches pubkey value from your wallet.dat file.

What's the use of public key ?

Public key is used to verify signatures created by its mathematically associated private key.

Address's Private key

If you want to get the private key -in wallet import format- of an address, use dumpprivkey method

```
dumpprivkey <address>
```

Note that, this method require unlocked wallet. Use walletpassphrase method to unlock your wallet and store the wallet decryption key in memory for <timeout> seconds

```
walletpassphrase <passphrase> <timeout>
```

for more information on working with wallets, check Chapter 8: Wallets.

Here's an example:

```
# python
address = "mvCVuo5KcbuSWRCXgcFcnZAyKotoyoFbEw"
```

```
# unlock your wallet for 1 minute if it's locked
bitcoin.walletpassphrase("my password", 60)
#private key in wallet import format
privkey = bitcoin.dumpprivkey(privkey)
print privkey
```

What's the use of private key ?

Private key is used to sign data. Bitcoin Core client uses address's private key to sign transactions spending funds received on this address as a proof of ownership. If you own the private key, you own the address and the funds received on this address. So keep it secret in an encrypted wallet.

Account's Receiving Addresses

As you've seen getaccountaddress method create new address every time the previous address received bitcoins, and getnewaddress can associate arbitrary number of addresses to any account. To get all receiving addresses associated with an account, use getaddressesbyaccount method:

```
getaddressesbyaccount <account>
```

where <account> is the name of the account, it will return an empty list if there's no such account name or if account is associated with no addresses in odd cases as we will see in the discussion of move method the next chapter, and it will return a list of all receiving addresses associated with <account> if it does exist:

```
bitcoin-cli getaddressesbyaccount "foo"
```

will return something like:

```
["address1", "address2", ...]
```

Getting Account of an Address

If you want to get the name of the account associated with an address use getaccount method:

```
getaccount <address>
```

where <address> is the bitcoin receiving address:

```
bitcoin-cli getaccount "mkwMkWEVTJDe6Qkb7SE3nLwYSfLChotwxj"
```

will return "" the name of the default account.

getaccount method like all other methods that deals with bitcoin addresses, if you call it with invalid address like 123456 , it will return "Invalid Bitcoin address" error with code -5.

Another issue to keep in your mind is that calling getaccount on foreign address that isn't in your local wallet will return "" empty string! this is the name of the default account. The solution to this problem is to validate the address using validateaddress method and making sure that it's in your local wallet.

Validate Bitcoin Address

You can check the validity of an address using validateaddress method:

```
validateaddress <address>
```

where <address> is the bitcoin address, it will return an object with these properties:

1) address - the address you're validating.

2) account - account associated with this address

3) isvalid - true if address is valid, false otherwise.

4) ismine - true if address is in your local wallet and you've its private key, false if foreign one.

5) iscompressed – true if address's public key is compressed.

6) isscript – if address is script hash, i.e: multi-sig address.

7) pubkey - the public key from which this address was derived.

8) redeemScript – if address is script hash, redeemScript will contain the script needed to spend funds on this address.

Here's an example:

```python
# python
addr = "31uEbMgunupShBVTewXjtqbBv5MndwfXhb"
bitcoin.validateaddress(addr)
```

will return:

```
{
    "isvalid" : true,
    "address" : "31uEbMgunupShBVTewXjtqbBv5MndwfXhb",
    "ismine" : false
```

```
            }
```

As you can see in the previous output, address 31uEbMgunupShBVTewXjtqbBv5MndwfXhb is perfectly valid bitcoin address but isn't mine.

Another example:

```
    bitcoin-cli validateaddress 123456
```

will return:

```
    { "isvalid" : false }
```

Another example:

```
    # python
    addr = "mvCVuo5KcbuSWRCXgcFcnZAyKotoyoFbEw"
    bitcoin.validateaddress(addr)
```

will return:

```
    {
            'account': '',
            'address': 'mvCVuo5KcbuSWRCXgcFcnZAyKotoyoFbEw',
            'iscompressed': True,
            'ismine': True,
            'isscript': False,
            'isvalid': True,
            'pubkey':
            '02c00edf56427eb69c9fd70886bd5554e6aa9bb4f105d41415109
            6bdff6f1ec462'
```

```
    }
```

Note that if you're on testnet and trying to validate a valid address on the mainnet, it will return that the address is invalid. In other words valid addresses on testnet are invalid on mainnet and vise versa.

Changing Account-Address Association

Accounts and addresses are associated using getaccountaddress and getnewaddress methods as you've seen earlier. This bond can be dissociated and changed using setaccount method:

```
    setaccount <address> <account>
```

where <address> is the bitcoin address, and <account> is the name of the account. Coins previously received on <address> will be debited from the previous account balance and will be credited to the address's new account.

setaccount method will change accounts balance and the new account associated with the address can spend funds received on this address using sendfrom method.

Suppose that account A1 is associated with two addresses D1 & D2, account A2 is associated with address D3. Address D1 received 15 bitcoins, and address D2 received 25 bitcoins.

```
    Bitcoin-cli getbalance "A1"
    bitcoin-cli getbalance "A2"
```

will return 40 and 0 respectively.

```
Bitcoin-cli getaddressesbyaccount "A1"
bitcoin-cli getaddressesbyaccount "A2"
```

will return:

```
[D1, D2]
[D3]
```

respectively.

Let's associate address D2 to account A2 and see what will happen:

```
bitcoin-cli setaccount "D2" "A2"
```

let's check balances and receiving addresses of each account:

```
bitcoin-cli getbalance "A1"
bitcoin-cli getbalance "A2"
```

will return 15 and 25 respectively.

```
Bitcoin-cli getaddressesbyaccount "A1"
bitcoin-cli getaddressesbyaccount "A2"
```

will return:

```
[D1]
[D2, D3]
```

respectively.

Calling setaccount method on an address and an account that are already associated to each other, will create a new address and associate it to that account. So for example if account A3 is associated to address D4 :

```
bitcoin-cli setaccount "D4" "A3"
```

will create a new address D5 and associate it to A3.

```
bitcoin-cli getaddressesbyaccount A3
```

will return:

```
[D4, D5]
```

so be careful.

If your "receiving addresses" list contains 2 addresses only, one associated with the default account "", and one associated with account "Foo". If you associate default account's address to account Foo, a new address will be created and associated to the default account ! Why ? Because there should be at least 1 address associated with the default account, because sendtoaddress method debits the default account and coins generated from mining are credited to the default account.

Note that setaccount works on foreign addresses ! If you associate an account with foreign address, address will be added to your receiving addresses list, but you won't be able to spend funds received on this address because you don't have its private key ! You can check if the address is yours using validateaddress method before association.

Listing All Accounts

If you want to get all account names and their balances, use listaccounts method:

```
listaccounts [minconf=1]
```

which will return an object that has account names as keys and account balances as value, set [minconf] to 6 to get the confirmed balance, for example:

```
Bitcoin-cli listaccounts 6
```

will return something like:

```
{
        "": 65.877,
        "foo": 12.9987
        "bar": 20.448
}
```

Checking Account's Balance

You can check the balance of a specific account using getbalance method:

```
getbalance [account] [minconf=1]
```

where [account] is the name of the account. If [account] is not specified, it'll return the wallet's total available balance. If [account] is specified, returns the balance in the account. [minconf] is the number of the minimum confirmations, set it to 6 to get the confirmed balance, set it to 0 to get the confirmed balance + unconfirmed balance, subtract to get the unconfirmed balance, [minconf] default value is 1 if omitted.

```
Bitcoin-cli getbalance "" 6
bitcoin-cli getbalance "" 0
```

If you want to get the wallet's total balance, omit [account]:

```
bitcoin-cli getbalance
```

if you want to get the wallet's total confirmed balance, set [account] to the wildcard "*", and set [minconf] to 6:

```
bitcoin-cli getbalance "*" 6
```

If you call getbalance method with a name of an account that doesn't exist, it'll return 0.0 not an error and won't create new account.

Bitcoin Core client version 0.9.0 introduced getunconfirmedbalance which returns   the server's total unconfirmed balance.

```
Bitcoin-cli getunconfirmedbalance
```

Getting Received by Account and Address

Note that getbalance method returns the sum of bitcoin amount in all transaction categories (including received, sent, immature, generated, and moved), on the other hand getreceivedbyaccount method returns the sum of bitcoin amount in **received** transactions category only:

```
getreceivedbyaccount <account> [minconf=1]
```

If the default account "" received 110 bitcoins, sent 20 bitcoins using sendfrom method as we will discuss in the next chapter, got 25 generated bitcoins from mining:

```
bitcoin-cli getbalance ""
```

will return 115.0, this is the amount received minus the amount sent, on the other hand:

```
bitcoin-cli getreceivedbyaccount ""
```

will return 110.0, this is the amount received, it doesn't has be the same as account's balance.

Another method for checking balance is getreceivedbyaddress which return the bitcoin amount received by a given address with minimum confirmations condition :

```
getreceivedbyaddress <address> [minconf=1]
```

A more detailed version is listreceivedbyaccount method which returns an array of objects, each object contains three keys:

- account - name of the account of the receiving addresses.

- amount - total amount received by addresses associated with this account.

- confirmations - number of confirmations of the most recent transaction.

```
listreceivedbyaccount [minconf=1] [includeempty]
```

set [includeempty] to true to include accounts with 0 amount.

```
Bitcoin-cli listreceivedbyaccount 0 true
```

will return something like this:

```
[
    {
            "account": "",
            "amount": 89.5584,
            "confirmations": 12
    },
    {
            "account": "foo",
            "amount": 24.6844128,
            "confirmations": 6
    },
    {
            "account": "bar",
            "amount": 0.00000000,
            "confirmations": 0
    }
]
```

Another method is listreceivedbyaddress which is the same as listreceivedbyaccount except that the result is grouped by address:

```
listreceivedbyaddress [minconf=1] [includeempty=false]
```

set [includeempty] to true to include addresses with 0 amount:

```
bitcoin-cli listreceivedbyaddress 0 true
```

will return something like:

```
[
    {
            "account": "foo",
            "amount": 1,
            "address": "address1...",
            "confirmations": 12
    },
    {
            "account": "foo",
            "amount": 15,
            "address": "address2...",
            "confirmations": 75
    },
    {
            "account": "bar",
            "amount": 0.00000000,
            "address": "address3...",
            "confirmations": 0
    },
    {
            "account": "bar",
            "amount": 15.85475600,
            "address": "address3...",
            "confirmations": 8
    }
]
```

Bitcoin Core client version 0.9.0 added transaction ids array to the output of listreceivedbyaddress method, to indicate the transactions in which each address received funds:

```
[
    {
        "address" : "mqwbK1tpnN2f8X6yZwW2ZSqMGKjD8fyhoy",
        "account" : "Foo",
        "amount" : 0.32000000,
        "confirmations" : 1165,
        "txids" : [
            "c3ffb2732f4511f380010bd122a35fc6416101fc7c07
3a0ab4a16a39cbb5b4ed"
        ]
    },
    {
        "address" : "mveBRwjGDs5nQ4oofEhsb6y2W2bqmgeiSD",
        "account" : "Foo",
        "amount" : 2.00000000,
        "confirmations" : 1165,
        "txids" : [
            "eb707d6144e5d75666bfdb94852da9d2d7b808ba0f44
f3a936da6a761702b5d0"
        ]
    }
]
```

you can inspect these transactions using gettransaction and getrawtransaction methods as we will see in Chapter 5: Transactions.

Key pool

Bitcoin addresses and their corresponding public and private keys are pre-generated and stored in queue in wallet.dat file before usage, the default queue size is 100 entries, and can be changed using -keypool option. When you need a new address using getnewaddress or getaccountaddress methods, this address is taken out of the queue and a new one is created and appended to the end of the queue to maintain the queue size only if your wallet is unlocked.

For example if your key pool size is 100, you will have 100 pre-generated bitcoin addresses in your wallet, these addresses are invisible to the GUI client and aren't listed in the output of JSON-RPC methods that return addresses like getaddressesbyaccount method. If you created 5 new addresses (D1, D2, D3, D4, and D5) using getnewaddress method, 5 new addresses (D6, D7, D8, D9, D10) will be created and appended to the end of the queue to refill the pool to 100 unused entries. These new addresses will be used after the previous 100 addresses are taken out of the queue, so you need to schedule your wallet backup before new addresses are used. For example if your keypool=1000, backup your wallet after each 750 address generation, or sending bitcoins, why ? because sending bitcoins may generate new *change addresses* as you'll see in the next section.

key pool feature was introduced so that old wallet backups will have certain number of addresses that will be used in the future, so old backups will be valid for both prior transactions and several dozen future transactions.

Key pool refilling can be forced using keypoolrefill method, this method is almost usless if your wallet is not encrypted! because as i told you before key pool refilling is done automatically, consider this scenario where i renamed my wallet.dat file, why? so bitcoin-qt will create new empty wallet.dat file, and started bitcoin-qt with keypool=10:


```
bitcoin-qt -keypool=10
```


then i call getnewaddress method inside a loop to generate 1000 addresses

```python
# python
from bitcoinrpc.authproxy import AuthServiceProxy, JSONRPCException
bitcoin = AuthServiceProxy("http://rpcuser:rpcpass@ip:port")
try:
    for i in range(0, 1000):
        print bitcoin.getnewaddress()
except JSONRPCException as e:
    print e.error
    if e.error["code"] == -12:
        bitcoin.keypoolrefill()
```

this code won't raise any error, especially "keypool ran out of keys, call keypoolrefill first" error with code -12.

The above code will raise an error only if your wallet is encrypted, why ? because keypoolrefill method requires unlocked wallet, so it won't be called automatically after getting new address out of the key pool queue because it requires you to unlock your wallet first using walletpassphrase method. For more information on how to encrypt, lock and unlock your wallet, check Chapter 8: Wallets.

If you deleted or renamed wallet.dat and started a bitcoind instance with --printtoconsole command-line argument, you'll see this output explaining what's happening behind the scenes

```
init message: Loading wallet...
nFileVersion = 80600
Performing wallet upgrade to 60000
keypool added key 1, size=1
keypool added key 2, size=2
keypool added key 3, size=3
.

.

.
```

```
keypool added key 98, size=98
keypool added key 99, size=99
keypool added key 100, size=100
keypool added key 101, size=101
keypool reserve 1
keypool keep 1
wallet                        7742ms
```

100 keys are pre-generated the first time Bitcoin client starts, 1 address is taken out of the pool to be assigned to the default account, so a new key 101 is created to maintain the key pool size to 100 unused keys.

Change Addresses

Suppose that you have a single address D1, and you received 50 bitcoins on this address, then you send 30 bitcoins of this 50 bitcoins to address D2 that you don't own, what will happen to the remaining 20 bitcoins ? Bitcoin Core client will create a new *change address* D3 and will send the remaining 20 bitcoins to D3, and will not keep them in the old address D1.

```
D1–30→ D2
  –20→ D3
```

Change address is invisible to the GUI client. Why new address? to improve your anonymity and make it a bit difficult for other people to track how many bitcoins you have and where you're spending them.

In the next chapter you'll learn how to generate and use change addresses using getrawchangeaddress method and raw transaction API.

Address Groupings

listaddressgroupings method is the only addresses listing method that
return change addresses in its output, this method was introduced in
Bitcoin Core version 0.7, it's used by coin control to select transaction
outputs to send as inputs in new transactions, Bitcoin Core version 0.9
added graphical user interface for the coin control feature so that advanced
users can select transaction inputs themselves, to turn on coin control
feature in Bitcoin Core 0.9, from "settings" menu, select "options", then
open "Display" tab, and check "Display coin control feature (experts only)",
go back to the main Bitcoin Core window, open "Send" tab, and you'll find
coin control feature added to the top of the window, when you click
"Inputs..." button, coin control window will be opened as shown in the next
picture:

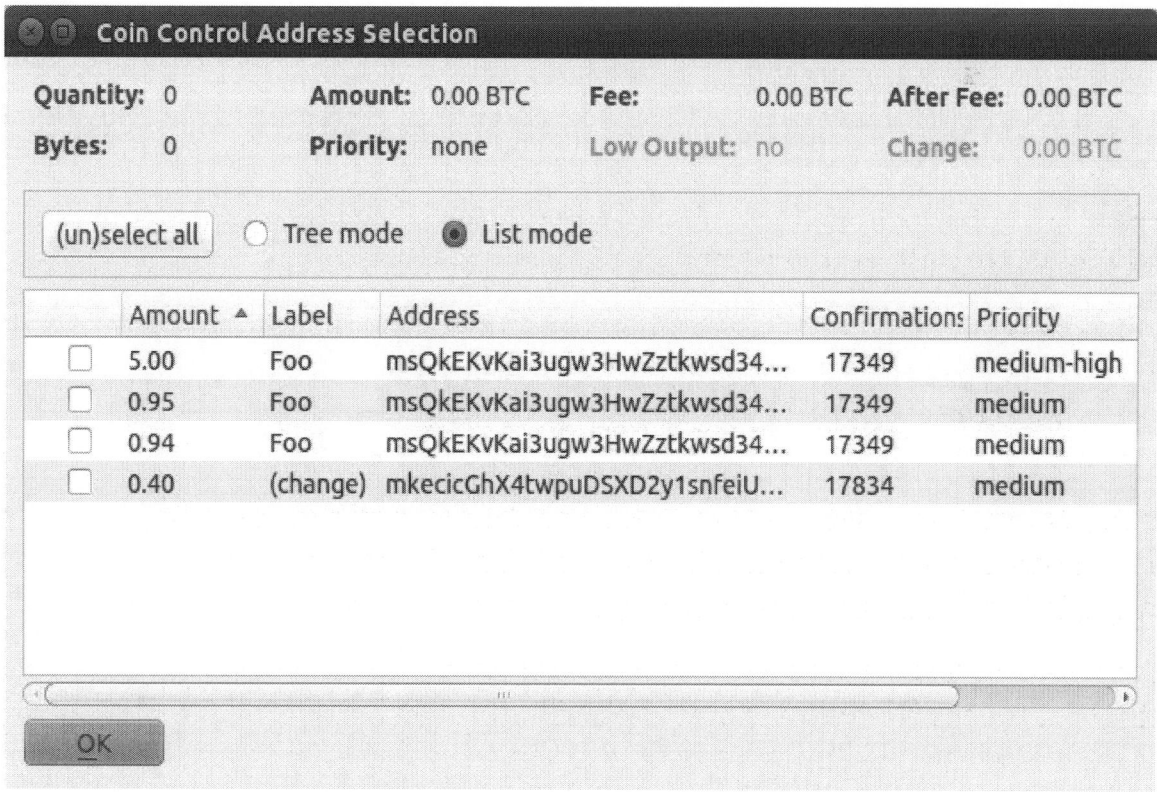

listaddressgroupings method accept no arguments and return addresses that has funds (transaction outputs) and its balance and the account name associated with it:

```
bitcoin-cli listaddressgroupings
```

will return:

```
[
    [
        [
            "mkecicGhX4twpuDSXD2y1snfeiUGLZ5MV6",
            0.40000000
        ],
        [
            "msQkEKvKai3ugw3HwZztkwsd34KNVCkU6J",
            6.89000000,
            "Foo"
        ]
    ]
]
```

If you have noticed, addresses in the output are the same as the addresses in the "coin control" window, I have more addresses, but these addresses are the only have funds.

Exit Address

Give your users the ability to enter an exit address, a bitcoin address that when something wrong like repeated login failure, her coins will be sent to this address. Exit address isn't a bitcoin feature, implement it yourself.

Archiving Addresses

Bitcoin receiving addresses can't be deleted ! Give your application users the ability to archive the addresses they are no longer using. In the addresses part of your application show them the addresses that aren't marked as archived, and let them select addresses and archive them. This is not a bitcoin feature, implement it yourself.

Vanity address

Vanity address is an address with specific words in it, it's like vanity car plates. Here's an example of vanity addresses:

```
1LoveRg5t2NCDLUZh6Q8ixv74M5YGVxXaN
1BoatSLRHtKNngkdXEeobR76b53LETtpyT
1NiNja1bUmhSoTXozBRBEtR8LeF9TGbZBN
1BTC24yVKQdQNAa4vX71xLUC5A8Za7Rr71
```

Vanitygen is a very fast command-line vanity address generator. Vanitygen accepts as input a pattern, regular expression, or list of patterns to search for, and produces a list of addresses and private keys. Vanitygen's search is probabilistic, and the amount of time required to find a given pattern depends on how complex the pattern is, the speed of your computer. For source code and full documentation goto https://github.com/samr7/vanitygen.

Here's a simple example of using vanitygen:

```
./vanitygen 1Boat
Difficulty: 4476342
Pattern: 1Boat
```

```
       Address: 1BoatX6pqMDNpAhs6jAY28kKnHH7PPBK3P
       Privkey:
5KbtFbZWn3nGTnHku9rxQQqkw1WLaCZVcKo4SZAP5cgRaJgZ7TF
```

To generate a testnet address pass -T option:

```
       ./vanitygen  -T moon
       Difficulty: 78508
       Pattern: moon
       Address: moonjbQGc9Zqf4sY1e3i87WEaddzQ5MtN8
       Privkey:
93Ho8wpQYPUXVcqxTf3en2x9jy3Hrhsc3Sj7hz7fd92YBgwmwqa
```

The longer the pattern, the more time it will take to find it.

Multi-signature (M-of-N) Address

Normal bitcoin address is associated with one private key, and who has access to this private key can spend funds received on this address, so if an attacker steal your *unencrypted* wallet, she will be able to spend all your funds because wallet contains your addresses and their private keys.

Multi-signature address is an address associated with more than one private key, these private keys can be owned by more than one person, i.e: you and . Just like any bitcoin address, multi-sig address can receive funds, but unlike normal bitcoin addresses, transaction that spend funds received on this address must be signed by you and i to be valid, so if an attacker steal your wallet, she couldn't send bitcoins associated with our multi-sig address to herself without my approval, and my approval here means signing the transaction by my private key, so she have to steal my wallet too ! My wallet is offline and i am from Egypt, where are you from ? and if she managed to steal our wallets, she may end up with two encrypted wallets, i guess she will suicide.

M-of-N address is a multi-sig address associated with N private keys, and the funds received on this address can be spent only if M private keys sign the transaction trying to spend those funds, where M >= N. (1 of 2), (2 of 2), (2 of 3) are example of valid Multi-sig address.

Note that at the time of writing this book, transactions spending funds received on multi-sig addresses with M <= 3 are valid and standard, multi-sig addresses with M > 3 are valid but not standard, standard transactions get relayed by Bitcoin nodes running standard bitcoin clients so won't be mined, non standard transactions don't. So if you want your non-standard (5 of 8) transaction to be mined, point your client to a mining pool who agree to process your transaction, and don't forget to include appropriate transaction fee.

Multi-sig (M-of-N) address can be created using createmultisig method:

```
createmultisig <nrequired> ["key1", "key2", ..."keyn"]
```

where <nrequired> is the number of signatures required to sign transaction spending funds received on this address, if you're creating 2-of-3 address, set <nrequired> to 2. <key>s is M bitcoin addresses or their corresponding public keys used to generate the multi-sig address, 2-of-3 address is generated from 3 keys.

If you specify <key>s as bitcoins addresses, these addresses must be in your local wallet, because createmultisig method will search for the public key for each bitcoin address in your local wallet, so if you give it foreign address like mimoZNLcP2rrMRgdeX5PSnR7AjCqQveZZ4 you'll get "no full public key for address mimoZNLcP2rrMRgdeX5PSnR7AjCqQveZZ4" error with code -1.

Here's an example of creating 2-of-3 address:

```
# python
addr1 = bitcoin.getnewaddress()
```

```
        # mkV5v6EVPZGooKoS1qBUbDkdDK3YtbkhaF
        adde2 = bitcoin.getnewaddress()
        # mjrdUThZe17PHAzLxCtam6gFxMhGnEUVBw
        addr3 = bitcoin.getnewaddress()
        # myYTEguZ7j5uAswa5MrZT45jTdEmikV3BN
```

at this point we have 3 address, in real world these addresses shouldn't be in the same wallet. The next step is to get the public key of each address:

```
        # python
        def pubkeyFrom(addr):
                res = bitcoin.validateaddress(addr)
                return res["pubkey"]

        pubkey1 = pubkeyFrom(addr1)
#
033b0d395f522a4c8c7425f68667ff8c775c053bf9f0ed8561ae6ce86d528cf7
92
        pubkey2 = pubkeyFrom(addr2)
#
032aa3bb6c74daa4bea37f8bf7a386fcde31c3732fddba66dc231335cd84b3b5
ca
        pubkey3 = pubkeyFrom(addr3)
#
02aaf0e592677105435d647c5508a75d8a93bb92c4bd530a57df23a987680baa
eb
```

In real world, users exchange their public keys using email or through web wallet supporting multi-sig addresses.

The final step is to use createmultisig method and give it the number of required signatures and our public keys:

```
        multisig = bitcoin.createmultisig(2, [pubkey1, pubkey2,
```

```
pubkey3])
    print multisig
```

If every thing is fine, createmultisig method will return an object with two properties address and redeemScript:

```
{
    'address': '2MvDsu5o56NRqjwqbBo8a21TXXXSLgbNUzr',
    'redeemScript':
'5221033b0d395f522a4c8c7425f68667ff8c775c053bf9f0ed8561ae6c
e86d528cf79221032aa3bb6c74daa4bea37f8bf7a386fcde31c3732fddb
a66dc231335cd84b3b5ca2102aaf0e592677105435d647c5508a75d8a93
bb92c4bd530a57df23a987680baaeb53ae'
}
```

Congratulations, you've just created your first multi-signature (2-of-3) address 2MvDsu5o56NRqjwqbBo8a21TXXXSLgbNUzr. We'll use redeemScript in the next chaper to spend funds received on our multi-sign address. Send some testnet bitcoins to this address and in the next chapter you'll learn how to spend those funds.

Multi-sig Address created by createmultisig method won't be associated to any account, won't be listed in your "receiving addresses" list in bitcoin-qt, and you won't receive notifications from Bitcoin-qt or -walletnotify as we will see in Chapter 9: Notifications when this address receive funds.

Use addmultisigaddress method if you want to asssociate your multi-sig address to an account specified by the last argument to this method or if you want to receive notifications from this address, note that addmultisigaddress won't add this address/account to your "receiving addresses" list , but it'll be shown in listaccounts method output:

```
    bitcoin.addmultisigaddress(2, [pubkey1, pubkey2, pubkey3],
"Multi")
```

you can verify that the address has been created and associated to "Multi"
account by:


```
bitcoin-cli listaccounts
bitcoin-cli getaddressesbyaccount "Multi"
```


listaccounts method will list all accounts in your wallet, and will show
"Multi". getaddressesbyaccount will return our multi-sig address.

Chapter 5: Transactions

Sending bitcoins from GUI like Bitcoin Core or an online wallet like blockchain.info is very simple, simply you type the bitcoin amount you want to send, and type or scan the QR code of the receiving address you want to send to. If you have sufficient balance in your account, a new transaction will be created -behind the scenes- signed and broadcast to the network, miners will process the transaction and add it to a block, each block appended to the block chain after this block is +1 confirmation. When 5 blocks are found after this transaction's block, its amount is added to the receiver's confirmed balance , the receiver of the bitcoins can spend them.

In this chapter we will discuss every RPC method involved with sending bitcoins. We will classify them into high-level methods and low-level methods. High-level methods are sendtoaddress, sendfrom, sendtomany, and move. Low-level methods are Raw Transaction API methods. High-level methods are very easy like the GUI, you simply give them the amount you want to send, the account you want to debit and the address(es) you want to send to. Raw transaction API was introduced in Bitcoin Core client version 0.7.0, it gives developers and very sophisticated end-users low-level access to transactions creation and broadcast. Raw transaction API is a little harder but gives you control over the whole process, you'll select the coins -transaction outputs- you want to spend by yourself, create raw transaction, set transaction fees, generate change address, sign the transaction, and broadcast it to the network until it gets into a block.

"Sending Bitcoins" is a bit vague description, actually nothing is sent ! what really happens is that the ownership is transfered, how ? If you have 5 bitcoins, and sent 3 out of them to your friend, the ownership of 3 bitcoins transfered from you to your friend. Proof of ownership is recorded in the blockchain, so no one can spend somebody's else coins as we will see later in **Transaction Verification** section.

Sending bitcoins require unencrypted wallet. If your wallet is encrypted, use walletpassphrase method to unlock the wallet and store the wallet decryption key in memory for <timeout> seconds.

```
# unlock your wallet for 1 minute
bitcoin.walletpassphrase("yourpassphrase", 60)
```

For more information on how to unlock your wallet, check Chapter 8: Wallets.

Sending From a Specific Account

Use sendfrom method if you want to send bitcoins from a specific account. "from account" here means spending funds received on this account's addresses.

```
sendfrom <account> <address> <amount> [minconf=1] [comment]
[comment-to]
```

where <account> is the account to debit, <address> is the bitcoin address of the receiver, <amount> is the bitcoins amount in real and rounded to 8 decimal places, [minconf] is the minimum confirmations used to ensure that account has sufficient funds,[comment] and [comment-to] are stored as text with the transactions in wallet.dat and not transmitted to the network, where [comment] is intented to store what the transaction is used for, and [comment-to] is used to store the name of the person you're sending the bitcoins. If <account> has sufficient funds greater than or equal to <amount> and <address> is a valid bitcoin address, a new transaction will be created, a new change address will be created to receive change if any, signed, and the transaction will be broadcast to the bitcoin network -behind the scenes, and transaction ID will be returned. If account has insufficient funds, an error with code -6 will be returned indicating that account has insufficient funds. Set [minconf] to 6 to spend confirmed transaction outputs because spending unconfirmed outputs may take a lot of time to confirm.

```
       Bitcoin-cli sendfrom "foo"
"mimoZNLcP2rrMRgdeX5PSnR7AjCqQveZZ4" 3.0
```

this example will send 3.0 bitcoins from account foo to the address mimoZNLcP2rrMRgdeX5PSnR7AjCqQveZZ4 and will return transaction id if successful.

Note that i am on testnet, if you tried the same code on mainnet you'll get "Invalid Bitcoin address" error with code -5.

```
       bitcoin-cli sendfrom "foo"
"mimoZNLcP2rrMRgdeX5PSnR7AjCqQveZZ4" 999.5
```

this will return an error with code -6 because i don't have 999.5 bitcoins in account foo, i wish i had.

If you're trying to send from an account that doesn't exist, you'll get "Account has insufficient funds" error with code -6.

If you send to an invalid address, you'll get "Invalid Bitcoin address" error with code -5.

sendfrom method select transaction outputs sent to <account>'s addresses and don't mess with other accounts' coins.

Sending From the Default Account

If you want to send from the default account "", use sendtoaddress method:

```
sendtoaddress <address> <amount> [comment] [comment-to]
```

for example:

```
bitcoin-cli sendtoaddress
"mimoZNLcP2rrMRgdeX5PSnR7AjCqQveZZ4" 3.0
```

which is equivalent to:

```
bitcoin-cli sendfrom ""
"mimoZNLcP2rrMRgdeX5PSnR7AjCqQveZZ4" 3.0
```

sendtoaddress method doesn't accept [minconf] parameter, which means that it can send unconfirmed transaction outputs if confirmed transaction outputs are insufficient. This will lead to a chain of dependency between unconfirmed transactions and confirmation delay, to solve this problem call getbalance method on the default account with 6 confirmations before using sendtoaddress method. For example if you want to send 4 bitcoins from the default account using sendtoaddress method, make sure that getbalance("", 6) is greater than or equal to 4.

```
if bitcoin.getbalance("", 6) >= amount:
    # safely send amount using sendtoaddress method
```

Bitcoin Core client version 0.9.0 introduced -nospendzeroconfchange command-line option to avoid spending unconfirmed change outputs.

Send Many

If you want to pay lots of people, it's more efficient to pay them with one big transaction using sendmany method rather than lots of little transactions:

```
sendmany <from-account> {address:amount, ...} [minconf=1]
[comment]
```

for example:

```
bitcoin-cli sendmany "POOL"
{"mimoZNLcP2rrMRgdeX5PSnR7AjCqQveZZ4": 3.0,
"mx3JLLeGSfEkcg3VEGZ2J3VFD18KdP2B9A": 1.0,
"mwbv6TqNNvSEba9cDYEWS1UGCDNJJy6fob": 2.0}
```

will return the transaction id:

```
73f4bf4aa22f50cee7d3daf661705f88b8577ce756e4faa541cfc28ee9645d91
```

this is the same as using sendfrom method 3 times:

```
bitcoin-cli sendfrom "POOL"
"mimoZNLcP2rrMRgdeX5PSnR7AjCqQveZZ4" 3.0
bitcoin-cli sendfrom "POOL"
"mx3JLLeGSfEkcg3VEGZ2J3VFD18KdP2B9A" 5.0
bitcoin-cli sendfrom "POOL"
"mwbv6TqNNvSEba9cDYEWS1UGCDNJJy6fob" 4.0
```

sendtomany will return the transaction id if successful, only one transaction will be created regardless of the number of the addresses.

The Evil "move"

Don't use move method.

You can adjust balance of your local wallet's accounts using move method:

```
move <from-account> <to-account> <amount> [minconf=1]
[comment]
```

where <from-account> is the account whose balance will be decremented, <to-account> is the account whose balance will be incremented, <amount> is real and rounded to 8 decimal places.

```
Bitcoin-cli move "foo" "bar" 10
```

this example will decrement foo's balance by 10 and increment bar's balance by 10, and may result in accounts with negative balance.

If you set <amount> to <= 0, you'll get "Invalid amount" error with code -3.

If you set <from-account> or <to-account> to name of an account that doesn't exist, a new account will be created without any associated addresses ! for example if gogo and zozo accounts doesn't exits:

```
bitcoin-cli move "gogo" "zozo" 3
```

will lead to this chain of events:

- account gogo will be created, without receiving address.

- account zozo will be created, without receiving address.

- set gogo's balance to -3.

- set zozo's balance to 3.

If you have two accounts, the default account "" and "Foo" account, and each account received 4 bitcoins on its associated address. If you used move method to adjust balance of Foo and "":

```
bitcoin-cli move "Foo" "" 4
```

this will make default account's balance 8, and Foo account's balance 0, and you won't be able to spend Foo funds using sendfrom method:

```
addr = "mimoZNLcP2rrMRgdeX5PSnR7AjCqQveZZ4"
bitcoin.sendfrom("Foo", 4)
```

will retrrun "Account has insufficient funds" error with code -6, although account Foo's address received 4 bitcoins earlier, but move method changed its balance to 0, and methods like sendfrom <account> check the balance of <account> before sending to make sure <account> has sufficient funds.

Even worse, the default account "" can spend Foo's funds !

```
addr = "mimoZNLcP2rrMRgdeX5PSnR7AjCqQveZZ4"
bitcoin.sendfrom("", addr, 8)
```

will work and return the transaction id.

Don't use move method.

Transaction Anatomy

A transaction is a digitally signed message that's broadcast to the bitcoin network, and included into blocks by miners. Transaction consists of one or more input and one or more output.

Transaction Input

Transaction input is a reference to a previous transaction output. Previous transaction output is referred to by the previous transaction's *transaction id* and the zero-based *index* of this output in the previous transaction, because each transaction can have multiple outputs. Only the owner of the output can spend it. Proof of ownership of output is achieved by including script in the input that references this output to satisfies the claiming condition found in the output as we will see in **Transaction Verification** section.

When you want to send 50 bitcoins to address D, you create a new transaction and reference previous *unspent* transaction output(s) that has value greater that on equal to 50 –these output(s) will be selected for you if you're using Bitcoin Core GUI or using high-level methods for sending bitcoins such as sendfrom, the result of this transaction is a new transaction output with value 50 credited to address D, and the transaction outputs that have been used as inputs in this transaction are marked as *spent*, and can't be spent again. Only the owner of address D can spend this output in a new transaction.

Transaction Output

An output contains instructions for sending bitcoins. Each *unspent* transaction output has value that will be worth when spent. Output is associated with bitcoin address. Owner of the address -who have its private key- can spend this output by referencing it in a new transaction as input. Each output has a claiming condition encoded in its script that should be satisfied by the input that references it to proof its ownership as we will see in **Transaction Verification** section. Your wallet's balance is the sum of all *unspent* transaction outputs value associated with the addresses in your wallet.

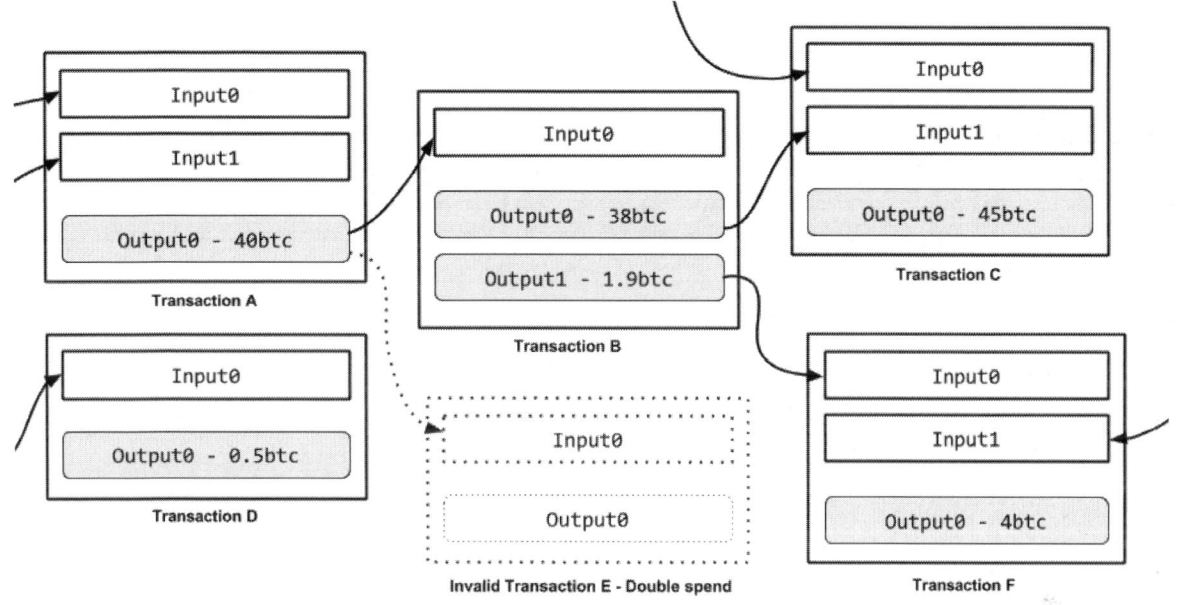

Each transaction output can be spent once, any attempt to spend transaction output twice -double spending- will result in invalid transaction as transaction E in the picture above. Unspent transaction outputs -indicated in the previous picture with gray rounded rectangles with no outgoing arrows- can be used as inputs in a new transaction or can be hold until 1 bitcoin equal 1 million dollars. You can't spend transaction outputs that you don't own, Bitcoin uses a stack language similar to Forth programming language to make sure that you're the owner of the outputs that you're spending as will see in **Transaction Verification** section. The sum of outputs value must be less than or equal to the sum on inputs value. If the sum of outputs value is equal to sum of inputs value, transaction fee will be 0 and it will be processed by miners and included in block with low priority in comparison to transaction with transaction fees as we will see in **Transaction Fees** section. If the sum of outputs value is less than the sum of inputs value, the difference will be transaction fee. If the sum of outputs value is greater than the sum of inputs value, transaction will be invalid. Transaction B in the previous picture has one input with 40 bitcoins, and has two outputs: one with 38 bitcoins and the other with 1.9 bitcoins, the difference between inputs and outputs 0.1 bitcoins will be used as transaction fees.

If you want to take a look at real transactions, http://blockexplorer.com and https://blockchain.info are your friends.

Information About Transactions

Let's send 1 bitcoin using high-level method like sendtoaddress methods which will return transaction ID, then check this transaction details using getrawtransaction method:

```
getrawtransaction <txid> [verbose=0]
```

which takes <txid> transaction id and optional [verbose] parameter with default value 0 if omitted. If verbose is omitted it'll return hex-encoded representation of the transaction. If verbose is non-zero, it will return an object with detailed information about transaction inputs and outputs.

```
addr = "mimoZNLcP2rrMRgdeX5PSnR7AjCqQveZZ4"
txid = bitcoin.sendtoaddress(addr, 1)
```

this will send 1 bitcoin to the specified address and will return the transaction id:

```
c5315f76c3d386726fc502fdbedea321deb71b4b68e92be37229b55221f410f8
```

If you called getrawtransaction method without verbose parameter:

```
hex = bitcoin.getrawtransaction(txid)
```

you'll get the hex-encoded transaction:

```
0100000001b9d3398885a7ce8f29bb42afdc98732d7a3cd11a9f3e57814e5406
81a5836114010000006b48304502201fd8abb11443f8b1b9a04e0495e0543d05
611473a790c8939f089d073f90509a022100f4677825136605d732e2126d09a2
d38c20c75946cd9fc239c0497e84c634e3dd012103301a8259a12e35694cc22e
bc45fee635f4993064190f6ce96e7fb19a03bb6be2ffffffff0200e1f5050000
00001976a91423b7530a00dd7951e11791c529389421c0b8d83b88ac802b530b
000000001976a9149b531d013b69500b1e2c08ede4855f81e9824a0288ac0000
0000
```

which can be decoded using decoderawtransaction method:

```
tx = bitcoin.decoderawtransaction(hex)
```

Finally call getrawtransaction on our transaction id, with verbose=1:

```
# equal to bitcoin.decoderawtransaction(hex)
bitcoin.getrawtransaction(txid, 1)
```

will return:

```
{
    "txid" :
    "c5315f76c3d386726fc502fdbedea321deb71b4b68e92be37229b55221
    f410f8",
    "version" : 1,
```

```
"locktime" : 0,
"vin" : [
    {
        "txid" :
        "146183a58106544e81573e9f1ad13c7a2d7398dcaf42bb29
        8fcea7858839d3b9",
        "vout" : 1,
        "scriptSig" : {
            "asm" :
            "304502201fd8abb11443f8b1b9a04e0495e0543d056
            11473a790c8939f089d073f90509a022100f46778251
            36605d732e2126d09a2d38c20c75946cd9fc239c0497
            e84c634e3dd01
            03301a8259a12e35694cc22ebc45fee635f499306419
            0f6ce96e7fb19a03bb6be2",
            "hex" :
            "48304502201fd8abb11443f8b1b9a04e0495e0543d0
            5611473a790c8939f089d073f90509a022100f467782
            5136605d732e2126d09a2d38c20c75946cd9fc239c04
            97e84c634e3dd012103301a8259a12e35694cc22ebc4
            5fee635f4993064190f6ce96e7fb19a03bb6be2"
        },
        "sequence" : 4294967295
    }
],
"vout" : [
    {
        "value" : 1.00000000,
        "n" : 0,
        "scriptPubKey" : {
            "asm" : "OP_DUP OP_HASH160
            23b7530a00dd7951e11791c529389421c0b8d83b
            OP_EQUALVERIFY OP_CHECKSIG",
            "hex" :
            "76a91423b7530a00dd7951e11791c529389421c0b8d
            83b88ac",
```

```
                    "reqSigs" : 1,
                    "type" : "pubkeyhash",
                    "addresses" :
                    ["mimoZNLcP2rrMRgdeX5PSnR7AjCqQveZZ4"]
              }
        },
        {
              "value" : 1.90000000,
              "n" : 1,
              "scriptPubKey" : {
                    "asm" : "OP_DUP OP_HASH160
                    9b531d013b69500b1e2c08ede4855f81e9824a02
                    OP_EQUALVERIFY OP_CHECKSIG",
                    "hex" :
                    "76a9149b531d013b69500b1e2c08ede4855f81e9824
                    a0288ac",
                    "reqSigs" : 1,
                    "type" : "pubkeyhash",
                    "addresses" :
                    ["mugEbbpEEJi7ZWZ5z9QPtoyzkzYkiKBsxp"]
              }
        }
    ]
}
```

if you're confused here's our transaction big picture:

```
{
      txid=
      version=
      locktime=
      vin=[input...]
      vout=[output...]
}
```

txid is our transaction id. version is the transaction versioning number for future enhancements and validation - current version is 1. locktime number will be discussed later in **Replacement Transaction** section. vin is array of transaction inputs. vout is array of transaction outputs.

Each input in the vin *inputs* array has this structure:

```
{
        txid=
        vout=
        scriptSig={
                asm=
                hex=
        }
        sequence=
}
```

txid is the transaction id of the previous transaction. vout is the zero-based index of this output in the previous transaction, don't confuse it with vout transaction outputs array. scriptSig "Script Signature" is used to prove that you're the owner of the outputs you're spending as inputs in this transaction and will be discussed in more details in **Transaction Verification** section. asm is the symbolic representation of the script. hex is the hexadecimal representation of the script. Hex-encoded script can be converted to asm using decodescript method as we'll see in **Transaction Verification** section. sequence number will be discussed in **Replacement Transactions** section.

Each output in the vout *outputs* array has this structure:

```
{
        value=
        n=
        scriptPubKey={
```

```
                    asm=
                    hex=
                    reqSigs=
                    type=
                    addresses=[address...]
        }
    }
```

value is the value of this output. n is zero-based index of this output in the vout array. scriptPubKey "Script Public Key" is used as claiming condition that should be satisfied to be able to spend this output in a new transaction and will be discussed in more details in **Transaction Verification** section. reqSigs is the number of the required signatures, spending funds from normal bitcoin addresses requires one signature, on the other hand spending funds received on multi-signature M-of-N address require M signatures. type is the type of the address, in this transaction it's a normal bitcoin address "hash of the public key" as indicated by "pubkeyhash", in transactions spending funds received on multi-sig address type is script hash, in coinbase transactions type is "pubkey".

Since Bitcoin Core version 0.8.0 a full index of historical transactions is no longer maintained, instead there's a database of unspent transaction outputs, getrawtransaction query this database, so if you tried to look up entirely spent transaction using getrawtransaction method, you'll get "No information available about transaction" error with code -5. If you want to explore historical transactions that maybe entirely spent, run bitcoind once with -txindex -reindex which will take sometime.

```
    Bitcoind -txindex -reindex
```

Another method for getting information about transactions is gettransaction -without raw:

```
gettransaction <txid>
```

where <txid> is transaction ID, it will return detailed information for **in-wallet** transactions, for example:

```
bitcoin.gettransaction("c5315f76c3d386726fc502fdbedea321deb
71b4b68e92be37229b55221f410f8")
```

will return:

```
{
        "amount" : -1.00000000,
        "fee" : 0.00000000,
        "confirmations" : 10730,
        "blockhash" :
        "00000000002c61dc09c617b041cd9af517e4ec1ee0adfb55f7342
        efbd35682f8",
        "blockindex" : 1,
        "blocktime" : 1393594981,
        "txid" :
        "c5315f76c3d386726fc502fdbedea321deb71b4b68e92be37229b
        55221f410f8",
        "time" : 1393594965,
        "timereceived" : 1393594965,
        "details" : [
            {
                "account" : "",
                "address" :
                "mimoZNLcP2rrMRgdeX5PSnR7AjCqQveZZ4",
                "category" : "send",
                "amount" : -1.00000000,
                "fee" : 0.00000000
            }
```

```
      ]
    }
```

where amount is the bitcoin amount i've sent in this transaction. fee is the transaction fee. confirmations is the number of blocks appended to the block chain after this transaction's block. blockhash is the hash of the block in which this transaction is included, you can get more information about this block using getblock method. blocktime is the time the block was created. blockindex is the 0-based index of this transaction in the block. time is the time this transaction was created. "time received" is the time your wallet learned about the transaction either by creating and broadcasting it if you're sending the transaction, or when it hits your wallet when you received a transaction. In the details array, account is the name of the account debited, address is the address i send the bitcoins to, category is the transaction category- in this case "send".

Listing Transactions

If you want to list all your in-wallet transaction, or transaction of specific account, use listtransactions method:

```
listtransactions [account] [count=10] [from=0]
```

which returns up to [count] most recent in-wallet transactions skipping the first [from] transactions for account [account], all parameters are optional, if [account] is omitted, it'll list all transactions for all accounts:

```
# list all transactions of the default account
bitcoin.listtransactions("")
```

will return something like this:

```
[
    {
        "account" : "",
        "address" : "mz2A28GQxWrYgMn2z9pRqaUFNqTMyhk1sJ",
        "category" : "receive",
        "amount" : 6.30000000,
        "confirmations" : 157,
        "blockhash" :
        "00000000befa3ef184f6c3cdec8814b945bad9e3f7ce9eb3
        8e3102bcf4c030c0",
        "blockindex" : 9,
        "blocktime" : 1397675516,
        "txid" :
        "f517350f088d235878ecab8d5241f0b6e59a4081eec22031
        c449d0d01d79ed66",
        "walletconflicts" : [
        ],
        "time" : 1397672026,
        "timereceived" : 1397672026
    },
    {
        "account" : "",
        "address" : "mz2A28GQxWrYgMn2z9pRqaUFNqTMyhk1sJ",
        "category" : "receive",
        "amount" : 6.30000000,
        "confirmations" : 148,
        "blockhash" :
        "00000000000146d6789357b60b41a8f853d0b188f90a1c66
        23657ccd26812b26",
        "blockindex" : 3,
        "blocktime" : 1397677533,
        "txid" :
        "659b00ea5b7dca1cb254ff625972a31ddbdf6363b803517a
        a030171dc861c596",
        "walletconflicts" : [
```

```
            ],
            "time" : 1397676663,
            "timereceived" : 1397676663
        }
    ]
```

In Bitcoin 0.9 walletconflicts is array of transaction ids that are conflicting with this transaction by spending the same outputs, conflicted transactions are reported with confirmation equal to -1.

If you want to list all your in-wallet transactions since a specific block, use listsinceblock method:

```
listsinceblock <blockHash>
```

where <blockHash> is the block hash, will return all transactions included in blocks after this block, or all transactions if <blockHash> is omitted.

Unspent Transaction Outputs

When you use higl-level methods like sendtoaddress method to send bitcoins, unspent transaction outputs are selected for you by automatic coin selection algorithm behind the scenes. But when using raw transaction API you will need to select unspent transaction outputs yourself. You can list unspent transaction outputs using listunspent method:

```
listunspent [minconf=1] [maxconf=9999999] ["address",...]
```

which returns an array of unspent transaction outputs between [minconf] and [maxconf] confirmations inclusive. Optionally filtered to only include transaction outputs paid to [address...]. All parameters are optional, the last parameter is array of addresses. for example:

```
    # list unspent transaction outputs with 6 minimum
confirmation
    bitcoin.listunspent(6)
```

will return something like this

```
    [
        {
            "txid" :
            "146183a58106544e81573e9f1ad13c7a2d7398dcaf42bb29
            8fcea7858839d3b9",
            "vout" : 1,
            "address" : "mkwMkWEVTJDe6Qkb7SE3nLwYSfLChotwxj",
            "account" : "",
            "scriptPubKey" :
            "76a9143b76312f1a174052cb717913b19b0ffbb25efb7d88
            ac",
            "amount" : 2.90000000,
            "confirmations" : 2813
        }
    ]
```

where txid is the transaction id. vout is the zero based index of this output in the transaction because transaction my have more than one output. address is bitcoin address that received the bitcoins. account is the name of the account associated with the receiving address - in this case it's the default account. scriptPubKey is the claiming condition that should be satisfied to spend this output and will be discussed later in **Transaction Verification** section. amount is the bitcoins amount in this transaction. confirmations is the number of blocks appended to the block chain after this transaction's block. This unspent transaction output can be used as input in a new transaction created by createrawtransaction method.

If you want to get information about a specific unspent transaction output, use gettxout method:

```
gettxout <txid> <n>
```

where <txid> is the transaction id, and n is the 0-based index of this output in the specified transaction, here's an example:

```
txid =
"659b00ea5b7dca1cb254ff625972a31ddbdf6363b803517aa030171dc861c59
6"
bitcoin.gettxout(txid, 0)
```

will return

```
{
        "bestblock" :
        "00000000755d314d3072586941e19597a8a4632effdf92421bf8d
        e7af7ff3ac4",
        "confirmations" : 160,
        "value" : 6.30000000,
        "scriptPubKey" : {
            "asm" : "OP_DUP OP_HASH160
            caf81d671c3454de47ab092af395787e66d444be
            OP_EQUALVERIFY OP_CHECKSIG",
            "hex" :
            "76a914caf81d671c3454de47ab092af395787e66d444be88
            ac",
            "reqSigs" : 1,
            "type" : "pubkeyhash",
            "addresses" : [
                    "mz2A28GQxWrYgMn2z9pRqaUFNqTMyhk1sJ"
```

```
                  ]
          },
          "version" : 1,
          "coinbase" : false
  }
```

where bestblock is the hash of the block in which this transaction with <txid> is included. coinbase is a boolean indicating whether it's a coinbase transaction or not. coinbase transaction is the first transaction in the block that give the miner 25 bitcoins plus the transaction fee of all transactions included in the block.

Calling gettxout method on spent transaction output will return nothing.

Another interesting method is gettxoutsetinfo, which accepts no arguments and returns statistics about the database of unspent transaction outputs that is maintained by a Bitcoin node:

```
  bitcoin-cli gettxoutsetinfo
```

will return something like:

```
  {
          "height" : 225494,
          "bestblock" :
          "00000000eb0443fd7dc4a1ed5c686a8e995057805f9a161d9a5a7
          7a95e72b7b6",
          "transactions" : 335344,
          "txouts" : 2221582,
          "bytes_serialized" : 72130407,
          "hash_serialized" :
          "3d14832b1b468f52ce942d4b9dc0c76a54fa6865207ff64540105
          403e3109f43",
          "total_amount" : 10886823.50380013
  }
```

where height is the height of the block up to which the set of unspent transaction outputs are accurate. bestblockhash is the hash of the block with that height. transactions is the number of distinct transactions to which unspent transaction outputs belong. txouts is the total number of unspent transaction outputs. hash_serialized is the hash of entire serialized database, you can use this value to compare with other nodes that are at the same block to verify the unspent transaction output set's integrity. bytes_serialized is how large the database in bytes. total_amount is the total amount of bitcoins in the unspent transaction outputs.

Locking Unspent Transaction Outputs

You can temporarily lock or unlock unspent transaction outputs, so they won't be selected by automatic coin selection when sending bitcoins using high-level methods like sendtoaddress method or using bitcoin-qt, and they won't appear in the output of listunspent method. Locked unspent transaction outputs are stored in memory, so if Bitcoin stopped, the locked outputs list will be cleared:

```
lockunspent <unlock?> [{"txid":txid, "vout": vout},...]
```

set <unlock?> to true if you want to unlock the specified transaction outputs, or set it to false to lock them:

```
#python
bitcoin.lockunspent(False, [{"txid":
"144320b63cbe0ff2333b4274ba3e0e4b7dabc17564659dfd76db11ce9aa1940
9", "vout": 0}])
```

Locking already locked output won't raise any errors.

Use listlockunspent method if you want to get a list of all temporarily locked unspent transaction outputs:

```
bitcoin-cli listlockunspent
```

will return something like this:

```
[{'vout': 0, 'txid':
'144320b63cbe0ff2333b4274ba3e0e4b7dabc17564659dfd76db11ce9aa1940
9' }]
```

If you locked all unspent transaction outputs and then tried to send some bitcoins using method like sendtoaddress you'll get "Insufficient Funds" error with code -4:

```
addr = "mimoZNLcP2rrMRgdeX5PSnR7AjCqQveZZ4"
utx = bitcoin.listunspent()
for u in utx:
    txid = u["txid"]
    vout = u["vout"]
    bitcoin.lockunspent(False, [{"txid": txid, "vout":
vout}])
    # this will raise error -4
    bitcoin.sendtoaddress(addr, 10)
```

Transaction Creation

Raw transactions can be created using createrawtransaction method:

```
createrawtransaction [{"txid": txid, "vout": vout},...]
{address:amount,...}
```

[ ] indicates array of objects not optional argument, where txid is the transaction id of the unspent transaction output. vout is its index. Both txid and vout can be found in listunspent method output. address is the bitcoin receiving address you want to pay. amount is the bitcoin amount. It will return the hex-encoded transaction as a string. Note that transaction inputs are not signed, transaction isn't stored in wallet.dat or transmitted to the network. There's no validity checks are done, so it's easy to create invalid transactions, transaction that double-spend, or transactions that won't be mined because insufficient transaction fee.

```
#python
hexrawtx = bitcoin.createrawtransaction([{"txid":
"659b00ea5b7dca1cb254ff625972a31ddbdf6363b803517aa030171dc861c59
6", "vout": 0}] , {"mimoZNLcP2rrMRgdeX5PSnR7AjCqQveZZ4": 5})
```

in this example we're spending 5 bitcoins from unspent transaction output with txid starting with 659b00ea... and index 0 which has 6.3 bitcoins to address starting with mimoZNLc... , the remaining 1.3 bitcoins will be used as transaction fee if we didn't receive the change in a change address. If everything is fine our transaction will be returned as hex-encoded string:

```
010000000196c561c81d1730a07a5103b86363dfdb1da3725962ff54b21
cca7d5bea009b650000000000ffffffff010065cd1d000000001976a91423b75
30a00dd7951e11791c529389421c0b8d83b88ac00000000
```

Receiving Change in Change Address

If you spend 8 bitcoins out of transaction output with 10 bitcoins amount, 2 bitcoins will be used as transaction fees unless you receive them in a change address. Starting in Bitcoin 0.9 you can generate a new change address using getrawchangeaddress method. Change addresses are invisible to Bitcoin-qt, you won't see them under "Receive" tab up to Bitcoin 0.8 or "Receiving Addresses" window in Bitcoin 0.9 , and aren't listed in the output of methods like getaddressesbyaccount.

```
#Bitcoin 0.9+ only
bitcoin.getrawchangeaddress()
```

will return:

```
mjvSXEySLWAPiqP4Cq9HPcUch9bbNBgWP6
```

lets change the transaction we created earlier to receive the change in our change address:

```python
#python
hexrawtx = bitcoin.createrawtransaction([{"txid":
"659b00ea5b7dca1cb254ff625972a31ddbdf6363b803517aa030171dc861c59
6", "vout": 0}] , {"mimoZNLcP2rrMRgdeX5PSnR7AjCqQveZZ4": 5,
"mjvSXEySLWAPiqP4Cq9HPcUch9bbNBgWP6": 1.2})
```

this will send 1.2 bitcoins to our change address starting with mjvSXEys... and the remaining 0.1 bitcoins will be used as transaction fee, and will return the transaction as hex-encoded string:

```
010000000196c561c81d1730a07a5103b86363dfdb1da3725962ff54b21
cca7d5bea009b650000000000ffffffff02000e2707000000001976a9143051a
21ec023fb778dad2ff1a1724084d2e35e0388ac0065cd1d000000001976a9142
3b7530a00dd7951e11791c529389421c0b8d83b88ac00000000
```

Signing Raw Transaction

Transactions created by createrawtransaction method can be signed using signrawtransaction method

```
signrawtransaction <hex_string> [{"txid": txid, "vout":
vout, "scriptPubKey": hex, "redeemScript": hex}...]
["privatekey"...] [sighash="ALL"]
```

where all arguments are optional except <hex_string> which is the hex-encoded transaction output from createrawtransaction method, other arguments are required if you're spending funds received on multi-sig address or funds received on an address whose private key isn't in the wallet. The second optional argument is an array of previous transaction outputs that this transaction depends on but may not be in the blockchain. The third optional argument is an array of base58check-encoded private keys that if given, will be the only private keys used to sign the transaction. The fourth optional argument is a string that specifies how the signature hash is computed https://en.bitcoin.it/wiki/OP_CHECKSIG. This method will return an object with two keys "hex" and "complete", where hex is the hex-encoded **signed** transaction, and complete is 1 or True if the transaction is completely signed, 0 or False if the transaction is partially signed in case of multi-sig transaction or not signed at all.

In the next example i sign the transaction that i've created in the previous section, i only call signrawtransaction with the hex-encoded transaction, i don't need to specify the private key of the address that has the funds, because the private key is in my wallet:

```
signed_rawtx =
```

```
bitcoin.signrawtransaction( "010000000196c561c81d1730a07a5103b86
363dfdb1da3725962ff54b21cca7d5bea009b650000000000ffffffff02000e2
707000000001976a9143051a21ec023fb778dad2ff1a1724084d2e35e0388ac0
065cd1d000000001976a91423b7530a00dd7951e11791c529389421c0b8d83b8
8ac00000000")
```

will return:

```
      {'hex':
'010000000196c561c81d1730a07a5103b86363dfdb1da3725962ff54b21cca7
d5bea009b65000000006b48304502210090be7161e35b8cb5d38612b3980949f
8d6f5104157151f83bd06aa5889155cce02205dd04736f42c1b73c01b42f7dbb
9c3000135ab95ee64da23f41ead5d14a007f101210271d2d4622b0b907e0c4d2
a3490eba6cb7cfda9150f1994b12371bc901b4ec91ffffffffff02000e2707000
000001976a9143051a21ec023fb778dad2ff1a1724084d2e35e0388ac0065cd1
d000000001976a91423b7530a00dd7951e11791c529389421c0b8d83b88ac000
00000', 'complete': True}
```

complete=True indicates that our transaction is completely signed, and hex
is the signed hex-encoded transaction that we can broadcast to the Bitcoin
network.

Broadcasting Transaction

After a transaction is created using createrawtransaction method, and
signed using signrawtransaction method, it's time to broadcast it to the
Bitcoin network using sendrawtransaction method:


```
sendrawtransaction <hex_string> [allowhighfees=False]
```

where <hex_string> is the signed hex-encoded transaction from signrawtransaction output. allowhighfees is a new optional parameter in Bitcoin 0.9 to allow high transaction fees, because Bitcoin 0.9+ rejects transactions with insanely high transaction fees. Bitcoin Core will reject any transaction with fees larger than 10000 * -minrelaytxfee, transaction fees will be discussed in more details in **Transaction Fees** section. Returns transaction id, or an error if the transaction is invalid for any reason. Bitcoin-qt/d will take care of re-transmitting the transaction periodically to the network until it's accepted into a block.

```
Bitcoin.sendrawtransaction("010000000196c561c81d1730a07a5103b863
63dfdb1da3725962ff54b21cca7d5bea009b65000000006b48304502210090be
7161e35b8cb5d38612b3980949f8d6f5104157151f83bd06aa5889155cce0220
5dd04736f42c1b73c01b42f7dbb9c3000135ab95ee64da23f41ead5d14a007f1
01210271d2d4622b0b907e0c4d2a3490eba6cb7cfda9150f1994b12371bc901b
4ec91ffffffff02000e2707000000001976a9143051a21ec023fb778dad2ff1
a1724084d2e35e0388ac0065cd1d000000001976a91423b7530a00dd7951e117
91c529389421c0b8d83b88ac00000000")
```

will return the transaction id:

e06604143c732a2d67c0609b9af3b7d79fe9b11b36aafde4a544361a336c4f78

Congratulations, you've created your first raw transaction, you should be happy :)

You can check our transaction using getrawtransaction method:

```
    bitcoin-cli getrawtransaction
"e06604143c732a2d67c0609b9af3b7d79fe9b11b36aafde4a544361a336c4f7
8" 1
```

or you can search for it on testnet block explorer here http://blockexplorer.com/testnet.

If you want to test double-spending, simply send the same signed transaction hex again, and you'll get "Transaction rejected" error. You'll get the same error if you tried to send unsigned or partially signed transaction.

Signing Mult-Sig Transaction

In this section we will create a multi-sig (2-of-3) address again, create a transaction that will send funds to this address, and another transaction that will spend funds received on it.

Create 3 receiving addresses:

```
addr1 = bitcoin.getnewaddress()
# mtFCSTrwm3zGfkeAyAYe4STP2vhGQYyAvP
addr2 = bitcoin.getnewaddress()
# muJayRQMBYkj6rzYTkHXRKa6cehm4MajEX
addr3 = bitcoin.getnewaddress()
# mfcuyQFKBJyKah3BkuJ9u4Da3i7CgoE1ot
```

Define a new function that extract public key from address:

```
def pubkeyFrom(addr):
    res = bitcoin.validateaddress(addr)
    return res["pubkey"]
```

Extract the public keys from addr1, addr2, and addr3:

```
    pubkey1 = pubkeyFrom(addr1)
#
038bfd8ed08f2adeeb63358a4f87e12a039ea75327a94cdce39487132b0849d7
8e
    pubkey2 = pubkeyFrom(addr2)
#
0380d7f6bba221647a12c2d02459bc7c08e7c6b081d5a0e070751f0cf0db4f1e
95
    pubkey3 = pubkeyFrom(addr3)
#
020247a6a40d2de8efc457902f91909e25cf2607ed4fa1a95305fef4d1276b69
6c
```

Create the multi-sig 2-of-3 address, where 2 is the number of required signatures to spend funds received on this address, and 3 is the number of keys associated with this address:

```
    bitcoin.createmultisig(2, [pubkey1, pubkey2, pubkey3])
```

which will return a 2-of-3 address and redeemScript:

```
    {'redeemScript':
'5221038bfd8ed08f2adeeb63358a4f87e12a039ea75327a94cdce39487132b0
849d78e210380d7f6bba221647a12c2d02459bc7c08e7c6b081d5a0e070751f0
cf0db4f1e95210380d7f6bba221647a12c2d02459bc7c08e7c6b081d5a0e0707
51f0cf0db4f1e9553ae', 'address':
'2MtH1MvE1gdzGqJTurP8ejEW1obipRX81nc'}
```

Lets fund our multi-sig address, select unspent transaction outputs:

```
    bitcoin.listunspent()
```

which will return unspent transaction outputs in my wallet:

```
[
    {
        "txid" :
        "bfa0bac35056d869c156fda638a7df36803e5823198d4264
        6e4a769896b2bb08",
        "vout" : 0,
        "address" : "mvrkLnk4ninN9xdY6RJUF9xsUCdifQ8cTB",
        "scriptPubKey" :
        "76a914a8483a6faf55360a1b90eeb9f1a12ec64dc55db088
        ac",
        "amount" : 21.00000000,
        "confirmations" : 266
    }
]
```

Create a new *funding transaction* spending 20.9 bitcoin of unspent transaction output with txid starting with bfa0bac... and vout 0 and amount 21 bitcoins as indicated in the listuspent output above, so 0.1 bitcoins will be used as transaction fee, :

```
hex = bitcoin.createrawtransaction([{"txid":
"bfa0bac35056d869c156fda638a7df36803e5823198d42646e4a769896b2bb0
8", "vout": 0}] , {"2MtH1MvE1gdzGqJTurP8ejEW1obipRX81nc": 20.9})
```

Sign the funding transaction:

```
signed_tx = bitcoin.signrawtransaction(hex)
hex = signed_tx["hex"]
```

which will return the signed hex-encoded transaction:

```
{"hex":
"010000000108bbb29698764a6e64428d1923583e8036dfa738a6fd56c169d85
650c3baa0bf000000006b48304502210092 69be2370fa3218d9e91fe4eadfca4
4522336c1257a1417cf585c61a1c9ce0f02202717b036f9bc2a714d4927b3961
cc4320d5fe3d1c3f876df377d955e2ab33dc10121034c27a414c9fab5b9ba4e8
5233d428752c26a91fa4847e071fefa4a729916624efffffff0180de927c000
0000017a9140b4e6acf54f5d908fcadab9e2d530545e05c55048700000000",
"complete": True}
```

Broadcast the signed hex-encoded transaction to the Bitcoin network:

```
txid = bitcoin.sendrawtransaction(hex)
```

which will return the transaction id:

```
ee65fc6429221ffed88ac65355302439d6126d767946784d880dcaee14d
4fae3
```

you can get the details of the transaction using getrawtransaction method:

```
bitcoin.getrawtransaction("ee65fc6429221ffed88ac65355302439
d6126d767946784d880dcaee14d4fae3", 1)
```

or search for the transaction in testnet block explorer
http://blockexprort.com/testnet.

Lets spend the funds -20.9 bitcoins- received on our multi-sig address:

```
multisig_hex = bitcoin.createrawtransaction([{"txid":
```

"ee65fc6429221ffed88ac65355302439d6126d767946784d880dcaee14d4fae
3", "vout": 0}], {"mimoZNLcP2rrMRgdeX5PSnR7AjCqQveZZ4": 20.8})

where txid is the id of the funding transaction that sent 20.9 bitcoins to our multi-sig address.

Sign the spending transaction using one private key. We will need txid, vout, and scriptPubKey from the output of getrawtransaction <txid>, where <txid> is the id of the funding transaction. We also need redeemScript from the output of createmultisig method above:

```
    # private key of the first address
    privkey1 =
bitcoin.dumpprivkey("mtFCSTrwm3zGfkeAyAYe4STP2vhGQYyAvP")
    # sign the transaction using 1 private key
    signed_multisig_tx = bitcoin.signrawtransaction(hex,
[{"txid":
"ee65fc6429221ffed88ac65355302439d6126d767946784d880dcaee14d4fae
3", "vout": 0, "scriptPubKey":
"a9140b4e6acf54f5d908fcadab9e2d530545e05c550487",
"redeemScript":
"5221038bfd8ed08f2adeeb63358a4f87e12a039ea75327a94cdce39487132b0
849d78e210380d7f6bba221647a12c2d02459bc7c08e7c6b081d5a0e070751f0
cf0db4f1e95210380d7f6bba221647a12c2d02459bc7c08e7c6b081d5a0e0707
51f0cf0db4f1e9553ae"}], [privkey1])
```

which will return:

    {'hex':
'0100000001e3fad414eeca0d884d784679766d12d63924305553c68ad8fe1f2
22964fc65ee00000000b40047304402200cf9eb4c1c2e6d756810a21b24e3349
da584532057491d93a130d513dec12b7d022016895295ff8f01cdb65e92f7689
fca5f50471d5201d3e43aa96770e1e7c8617f014c695221038bfd8ed08f2adee
b63358a4f87e12a039ea75327a94cdce39487132b0849d78e210380d7f6bba22

1647a12c2d02459bc7c08e7c6b081d5a0e070751f0cf0db4f1e95210380d7f6b
ba221647a12c2d02459bc7c08e7c6b081d5a0e070751f0cf0db4f1e9553aefff
fffff010048fa7b000000001976a91423b7530a00dd7951e11791c529389421c
0b8d83b88ac00000000', 'complete': False}

complete=False indicates that the transaction isn't completely signed, in real world the owner of the first address will send the partially-signed transaction hex to the owner of the second address to sign it with its corresponding private key:

```
hex2 = signed_multisig_tx["hex"]
privkey2 =
bitcoin.dumpprivkey("muJayRQMBYkj6rzYTkHXRKa6cehm4MajEX")
signed_multisig_tx2 = bitcoin.signrawtransaction(hex2,
[{"txid":
"ee65fc6429221ffed88ac65355302439d6126d767946784d880dcaee14d4fae
3", "vout": 0, "scriptPubKey":
"a9140b4e6acf54f5d908fcadab9e2d530545e05c550487",
"redeemScript":
"5221038bfd8ed08f2adeeb63358a4f87e12a039ea75327a94cdce39487132b0
849d78e210380d7f6bba221647a12c2d02459bc7c08e7c6b081d5a0e070751f0
cf0db4f1e95210380d7f6bba221647a12c2d02459bc7c08e7c6b081d5a0e0707
51f0cf0db4f1e9553ae"}],[privkey2])
```

At this point our transaction is signed using 2 private keys, and because it's spending funds received on 2-of-3 multi-sig address, it's now completely signed as indicated by complete=True in signed_multisig_tx2 value:

{'hex':
'0100000001e3fad414eeca0d884d784679766d12d63924305553c68ad8fe1f2
22964fc65ee00000000fdfd00000483045022100bfc0efe27c0af41ae32367007
af0cbf37fa83deccbed5ad3226c1fa92b8abb2f022039704bd0284031a3e1340
66492b535457792f1119ba343a6406417a45bf086b701473044022072d1d688c

566639125b28a8bcdff293bc4a53a8d3fd56985f6bbdbded5203444022011e1f
0aea0d88d1d2092b5be65ebe11bfcbdda85381792ce58f52bb10d81b859014c6
95221038bfd8ed08f2adeeb63358a4f87e12a039ea75327a94cdce39487132b0
849d78e210380d7f6bba221647a12c2d02459bc7c08e7c6b081d5a0e070751f0
cf0db4f1e95210380d7f6bba221647a12c2d02459bc7c08e7c6b081d5a0e0707
51f0cf0db4f1e9553aeffffffff010048fa7b000000001976a91423b7530a00d
d7951e11791c529389421c0b8d83b88ac00000000', **'complete': True}**

The final step is to broadcast it to the Bitcoin network using sendrawtransaction <hex_string> where <hex_string> is the hex-encoded completely signed transaction:

```
signed_hex = signed_multisig_tx2["hex"]
spending_txid = bitcoin.sendrawtransaction(signed_hex)
```

which will successfully broadcast our transaction and return the transaction id:

ad53a5d0c0ff1ad027f862556a760c6e629b41ebc46d482ad3a0319b63d027e1

you can verify it using getrawtransaction method or search for the transaction id on testnet block explorer http://blockexplorer.com/testnet

Transaction Verification

Bitcoin is using a stack scripting language like Forth to verify that you're authorized to spend transaction outputs in new transaction. Each transaction output has a claiming condition encoded in its scriptPubKey like "give me a signature i can verify with this public key", "give me the password" or "what's the sum of one and two", and the input that references this output must include a scriptSig that satisfies the referenced output's scriptPubKey, such that when scriptSig is executed followed by scriptPubKey, if the result is True, you're authorized to spend this output.

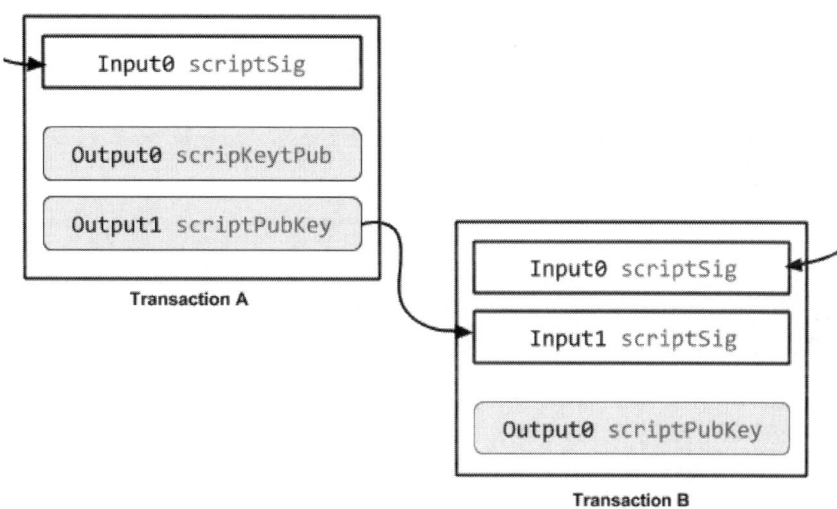

In the previous picture, Input1 in Transaction B references Output1 in Transaction A, Input1's scriptSig must provide what's needed by Output1's scriptPubKey. Bitcoin will execute scriptSig followed by scriptPubKey, if the result is True, you're authorized to spend Output1, otherwise the transaction is invalid.

If you're spending funds received on a normal Bitcoin address (public key hash), here are the scriptSig of the input and scriptPubkey of the referenced output:

scriptSig
<sig> <pubkey>

scriptPubKey

OP_DUP OP_HASH160 <pubKeyHash> OP_EQUALVERIFY OP_CHECKSIG

where <> indicates data pushed to the stack, and OP_* indicates functions that operate on stack data at the top. In scriptSig i provide a signature <sig> created by the private key of the address that received the funds, and provide the public key of the address <pubkey>. scriptPubKey verifies that <pubkey> hashes to the provided <pubKeyHash>, then checks the signature <sig> against the public key <pubKey>.

Here are the steps taken to execute this script:

Stack	Script	Description
Empty	<sig> <pubKey>	scriptSig
<sig>	<pubKey>	<sig> is pushed to the stack
<pubKey> <sig>	Empty	<pubKey> is pushed to the stack
<pubKey> <sig>	OP_DUP OP_HASH160 <pubKeyHash> OP_EQUALVERIFY OP_CHECKSIG	scriptPubKey
<pubKey> <pubKey> <sig>	OP_HASH160 <pubKeyHash> OP_EQUALVERIFY OP_CHECKSIG	OP-DUP duplicates top stack items
<pubKeyHash> <pubKey> <sig>	<pubKeyHash> OP_EQUALVERIFY OP_CHECKSIG	OP_HASH160 hashes top stack item <pubKey> to <pubKeyHash>, where OP_HASH160(X) = ripemd160(sha256(x))
<pubKeyHash>	OP_EQUALVERIFY OP_CHECKSIG	<pubKeyHash> is

<pubKeyHash> <pubKey> <sig>		pushed to the stack
<pubKey> <sig>	OP_CHECKSIG	OP_EQUALVERIFY checks that the top two stack items are equal. If they're equal execution continues. If they are not equal, False will be pushed to the stack and the script will end.
True	Empty	OP_CHECKSIG checks the signature <sig> using the public key <pubKey> and push True to the stack if <sig> was generated using the private key associated with <pubKey>

Another type of transactions is spending funds received on multi-sig address (script hash), here are scriptSig of the input and scriptPubKey of the referenced output of one-signature required 1-of-1 transaction for the sake of simplicity:

scriptSig:
<sig> {[pubkey] OP_CHECKSIG}

scriptPubKey:
```
OP_HASH160 [hash of {[pubkey] OP_CHECKSIG}] OP_EQUAL
```

Here are the steps taken to execute the script:

Stack	Script	Description
Empty	`<sig> {[pubkey] OP_CHECKSIG}`	scriptSig
`<sig>`	`{[pubkey] OP_CHECKSIG}`	`<sig>` is pushed to the stack
`{[pubkey] OP_CHECKSIG} <sig>`	Empty	script {[pubkey] OP_CHECKSIG} is pushed to the stack, later this script will be executed !
`{[pubkey] OP_CHECKSIG} <sig>`	`OP_HASH160 [hash of {[pubkey] OP_CHECKSIG}] OP_EQUAL`	scriptPubKey
`[hash of {[pubkey] OP_CHECKSIG}] <sig>`	`[hash of {[pubkey] OP_CHECKSIG}] OP_EQUAL`	OP_HASH160 hashes top stack item {[pubkey] OP_CHECKSIG}
`[hash of {[pubkey] OP_CHECKSIG}] [hash of {[pubkey] OP_CHECKSIG}`	`OP_EQUAL`	[hash of {[pubkey] OP_CHECKSIG}] is pushed from scriptPubkey to the stack

] `<sig>`		
`<sig>`	Empty	OP_EQUAL checks the top two stack values for equality. If they're not equal, False will be pushed to the stack and transaction will be invalid.

At this point <sig> is left in the stack and the scriptPubkey is empty !

A magic move will happen, remember {[pubkey] OP_CHECKSIG}] ? this this will be the new value of scriptPubKey ! Lets see what will happen:

Stack	Script	Description
`<sig>`	`<pubkey> OP_CHECKSIG`	scriptPubKey
`<pubkey>` `<sig>`	`OP_CHECKSIG`	`<pubKey>` is pushed to the stack
`True`	Empty	OP_CHECKSIG checks the signature `<sig>` using the public key `<pubKey>` and push True to the stack if `<sig>` was generated using the private key associated with `<pubKey>`

The final type of transaction we will look at is *coinbase transaction* (pay to public Key), the transaction that gives the miner who wins the hashing competition 25 bitcoins plus all the transaction fees of the transactions included in the block. Here are the scriptPubKey of the generation transaction output and the scriptSig of the transaction input of the transaction trying to spend it:

scriptSig:
```
<sig>
```

scriptPubKey:
```
<pubKey> OP_CHECKSIG
```

Here are the steps taken to execute the script:

Stack	Script	Description
Empty	<sig>	scriptSig
<sig>	Empty	<sig> is pushed to the stack
<sig>	<pubKey> OP_CHECKSIG	ScriptPubKey
<pubKey> <sig>	OP_CHECKSIG	<pubKey> is pushed to the stack
True	Empty	OP_CHECKSIG checks the signature <sig> using the public key <pubKey> and push True to the stack if <sig> was generated

		using the private key associated with <pubKey>

Bitcoin 0.9+ introduced decodescript method, which can be used to decode hex-encoded scripts:

```
decodescript <hex>
```

where <hex> is the hex encoded script:

```
hex = "76a91423b7530a00dd7951e11791c529389421c0b8d83b88ac"
bitcoin.decodescript(hex)
```

will return:

```
{
        "asm" : "OP_DUP OP_HASH160
        23b7530a00dd7951e11791c529389421c0b8d83b
        OP_EQUALVERIFY OP_CHECKSIG",
        "reqSigs" : 1,
        "type" : "pubkeyhash",
        "addresses" : [
             "mimoZNLcP2rrMRgdeX5PSnR7AjCqQveZZ4"
        ],
        "p2sh" : "2MsRE5jYEA51YBRATidAx8xHyZNvraVPRX2"
}
```

where asm is the symbolic representation of the script "OP_DUP OP_HASH160 <pubKeyHash> OP_EQUALVERIFY OP_CHECKSIG" where

\<pubKeyHash\> is 23b7530a00dd7951e11791c529389421c0b8d83b. reqSigs is the number of required signatures to spends funds received on this address. type is the transaction type, in this case it's "pay to public key hash". addresses is an array of addresses associated with the script, p2sh is the pay to script hash address of the given script.

remember our multi-sig address's redeemScript ?

```
bitcoin.decodeaddress(redeemScript)
```

will return

```
{
        "asm" : "2
        038bfd8ed08f2adeeb63358a4f87e12a039ea75327a94cdce39487
        132b0849d78e
        0380d7f6bba221647a12c2d02459bc7c08e7c6b081d5a0e070751f
        0cf0db4f1e95
        0380d7f6bba221647a12c2d02459bc7c08e7c6b081d5a0e070751f
        0cf0db4f1e95 3 OP_CHECKMULTISIG",
        "reqSigs" : 2,
        "type" : "multisig",
        "addresses" : [
                "mtFCSTrwm3zGfkeAyAYe4STP2vhGQYyAvP",
                "muJayRQMBYkj6rzYTkHXRKa6cehm4MajEX",
                "muJayRQMBYkj6rzYTkHXRKa6cehm4MajEX"
        ],
        "p2sh" : "2MtH1MvE1gdzGqJTurP8ejEW1obipRX81nc"
}
```

where asm is the script encoded in redeemScript "2 \<pubKey1\> \<pubKey2\> \<pubKey3\> 3 OP_CHECKMULTISIG". reqSigs is the number of required signature required to sign spending transaction that spend funds received on this address. type is the type of the transaction: spending funds of "multi-sig" address. addresses is array of the addresses associated with the multi-sig address. p2sh is the pay to script hash address of the given script.

Transaction Fees

Transaction fees is the difference between transaction inputs total amount and transaction outputs total amount. Fees go to the miners to incentivize them to keep mining and secure the bitcoin network. Transaction fees come into play in three events: sending bitcoins, relaying transactions, and including transactions in a block.

Sending Bitcoins

A transaction may be safely sent without transaction fees at all if these conditions are met:

1) Its size is smaller than 1,000 bytes

2) All outputs are 0.01 btc or larger

3) Its priority is larger than 57,600,000

How priority is calculated ?

```
    priority = sum(input value * confirmations) / transaction
size
```

where input value in satoshis , and transaction size in bytes, where 1 kilobyte = 1000 bytes.

For example, a transaction with two inputs, 4 bitcoins with 20 confirmations, and 3 bitcoins with 50 confirmation, and its size is 500 bytes, will have a priority of:

```
(400,000,000 * 20 + 300,000,000 * 50) / 500 = 46,000,000
```

which is lower than the high priority threshold 57,600,000 , so transaction fees per kilobyte is required. Transaction size will be rounded up to the nearest thousand bytes and add a fee per thousand kilobytes will be added.

Bitcoin Core Version	Transaction fees per 1000 bytes
before 0.8.2	0.0005 btc
0.8.2+	0.0001 btc (0.1 btc)
0.9.0+	0.00001 btc (0.01 mbtc)

For example, the previous transaction with 46,000,000 priority, its size is 500 kb, which will be rounded up to 1000 kb, so it needs 0.00001 btc as fees in Bitcoin Core 0.9.0+.

Including in Blocks

In each mined block there's 50,000 bytes reserved for highest-priority transactions regardless of transaction fees, another 700,000 bytes are reserved for transactions that pay at lease 0.00001 btc (0.01 mbtc) per kb where transactions with highest fee per kb are added first.

The remaining transactions remain in the miner's "memory pool" which can be accessed using getrawmempool method, these transaction may be included later in blocks if their priority or fee is large enough.

```
getrawmempool [verbose=false]
```

if verbose is omitted, it'll return an array of transaction ids of transactions that are in the memory pool. If verbose=true it'll return an object where each key is a transaction id and the value is a detailed object about the transaction:

```
bitcoin.getrawmempool()
```

will return:

```
[
    "0c3525fa2558b3fc92d818c00c63b8244202138fc1a708328f112
    1cff0b0854e",
    "1e601efd8319333ca35ff1e4dc595d8a82b919191538697f67ad2
    41f8ec6dfa5",
    "29b3d086e037e04a4dbb7473f3d3c91a62bf72c8a33e0876b96b7
    7a9fdfe51ff",
    "2d9257658758eef2cae094261517bf78668f9cbf390e3e210509a
    05d88fca1e6",
    ...
]
```

If you pass true to the getrawmempool method:

```
bitcoin.getrawmempool(True)
```

it will return:

```
{
    "0c3525fa2558b3fc92d818c00c63b8244202138fc1a708328f112
    1cff0b0854e" : {
        "size" : 226,
```

```
          "fee" : 0.00000000,
          "time" : 1398280435,
          "height" : 226284,
          "startingpriority" : 1370963835.43589735,
          "currentpriority" : 1370963835.43589735,
          "depends" : [
          ]
     },
  ...
}
```

where 0c3525f... is transaction id. size is the transaction size in bytes. fee is the transaction fee in bitcoins. time is the time transaction entered the pool in seconds since 1 Jan 1970 GMT. height is the block height when transaction entered the pool. startingpriority is the transaction priority when the transaction entered the pool. currentpriority is the transaction priority now. depends is an array of transaction ids of unconfirmed transactions used as inputs for this transaction.

Relaying

The fees required to relay the transaction across the Bitcoin network are the same as the transaction fees, 0.0001 btc/kb required by Bitcoin 0.8.2+ and 0.00001 btc/kb required by 0.9+, and can be changed using -minrelaytxfee option.

Transaction with transaction outputs of 0.543 times the minimum relay fee are considered non-standard since Bitcoin 0.8.2+ because storing them costs the network more than they are worth, and sending them will cost their owner transaction fees more than they are worth. So if you send 0.00005430 btc, Bitcoin nodes running Bitcoin 0.8.2 with default settings will refuse to relay it to its peers, fortunately nodes running Bitcoin 0.9+ will relay it, because Bitcoin 0.9+ minimum transaction fees dropped from

0.1 mbtc to 0.01 mbtc.

To prevent penny-flooding denial of service attack, nodes that run the standard bitcoin client limit free transactions that get relayed to its peer to 15 thousand bytes per minute, this setting can be changed using -limitfreerelay option.

Changing Settings

All the previous rules can be changed using command-line or bitcoin.conf settings summarized in the following table:

Setting	default value	use
paytxfee	0.0 btc per kilobyte	Fee per kilobyte for transactions you send
mintxfee	0.01 mbtc per kilobyte in Bitcoin Core 0.9.0+	Minimum fee per kilobyte of transaction to include in your blocks. Fees smaller than this are considered zero fee
minrelaytxfee	as -mintxfee	Minimum fee per kilobyte of transaction to relay to other nodes. Fees smaller than this are considered zero fee
limitfreerelay	15 kilobytes per minute	Size of free transactions in kilobytes per minute to relay to other nodes
blockminsize	0.0	Minimum size of the block

		created
`blockmaxsize`	750,000 bytes	Maximum size of the block created
`blockprioritysize`	250,000 bytes	Size of block for the highest-priority transactions

You can use `settxfee` method to set the fee per kilobyte for transactions you send at runtime:

```
bitcoin.settxfee(0.0001)
```

which will return True if successful.

Replacement Transactions

Each transaction has a "locktime" parameter, and each transaction input has a "sequence" parameter, both parameters are set automatically for you by Bitcoin-qt/d and there's neither a JSON RPC method nor an interface in Bitcoin Core client to change them. The only way to change them is to edit the raw transaction hex ! What are these parameters used for ?

locktime parameter is used to delay transaction inclusion in block until after a specific unix timestamp or block height after they are broadcast to the Bitcoin network. If locktime value is less that 500,000,000, then the transaction will not be included in a block until after a block with that absolute height value is reached. If locktime value is greater than or equal 500,000,000 then transaction will not be included in a block until after that unix timestamp value. Delayed transaction will be stored in the memory pool of the nodes until it's time to be included in a block.

For example, if you set locktime to the current block height + 3, transaction won't be included in a block until 3 blocks are appended to the blockchain, approximately after 30 minutes assuming that a block is found every 10 minutes. Default locktime value is 0, which means that transaction is final and won't be delayed.

sequence parameter is used to introduced a new version of the same delayed transaction, where transaction with higher sequence number will replace transaction with lower sequence number in the node's memory pool before they are included into a block. If all transaction inputs have final sequence value 0xffffffff (4294967295), then the transaction is final and locktime value is irrelevant.

If you're lost, here are the "finalness" rules:

- If all transaction's inputs have UINT32_MAX sequence value, then the transaction is final regardless of locktime.

- If transaction locktime (height or time) is in the past, the transaction is final.

Delayed and replacement transactions are non-standard, so they will be rejected and won't be relayed by the standard nodes because of the trivial denial-of-service attack they enable. An attacker can fill the network nodes' memory pool with delayed transaction that will take forever to be included in a block.

Bitcoin Core version 0.9.0+ will accept transactions with locktime that will finalize in the next block, i.e: transaction with locktime equal to current block height + 1.

Chapter 6: Notifications

Notification of Transactions

Bitcoin Core 0.8.2 introduced -walletnotify option, which can be used to execute a command when a transaction hits your wallet, %s in the command will be replaced with transaction id. You'll receive multiple notifications for each transaction, the first time is when you send or receive a transaction, and the second time when this transaction is included into a block.

For example, i added walletnotify to my bitcoin.conf file to register a python program, which will be executed when a transaction hits my wallet, and %s will be replaced with transaction id:

```
walletnotify=python ~/tx.py %s
```

in this example, i didn't specify the absolute path of python interpreter executable because it's in my PATH environment variable, and specified the absolute path of tx.py file. %s will be replaced with the transaction id.

Here's my simple tx.py file, which takes transaction id as command-line argument and append it to tx.log file:

```
# python
import sys

if len(sys.argv) > 1:
    txid = sys.argv[1]
```

```
    with open("tx.log", "a") as f:
        f.write(txid + "\n")
```

If your walletnotify doesn't work, make sure that what comes after walletnotify= works fine from the command-line, in my case:

```
python ~/tx.py 123456
```

will work fine and append 123456 to tx.log file.

Notifications of Blocks

Bitcoin Core 0.6.0 introduced -blocknotify option, which can be used to execute a command when the best block changes. The best block is the last block in the blockchain, the block with the highest height number. %s in the command will be replaced with the block hash.

```
blocknotify=python ~/block.py %s
```

-blocknotify can be used alongside with -walletnotify and getrawtransaction method to implement a block explorer.

Notification of Alerts

Bitcoin Core 0.8.2 introduced -alertnotify option, which can be used to execute a command when a relevant alert message is received from the Bitcoin network or when a long blockchain fork is detected, %s in the command will be replaced with the alert message.

```
alertnotify=python ~/alert.py %s
```

Until Bitcoin Core 0.3.2, when alert message was received, Bitcoin Core went to safe mode. In safe mode all JSON RPC methods that send bitcoins are disabled and return -2 error instead. Current versions no longer go into safe mode when alert is received. It's wise for Bitcoin wallets/service to disable withdrawal feature when alert is received and send SMS to developers to wake up and do something.

An example of recent alert is alert received on April 11, 2014 for Bitcoin 0.9.0 users to upgrade due to OpenSSL heartbleed bug, with relative priority 5000 which is very high compared to previous alerts.

Alerts are targeted to a specific Bitcoin versions, nodes higher or lower that the targeted versions will relay the alert to its peers. Call getinfo method when you receive alert notification and check errors field in the output:

```
bitcoin-cli getinfo
```

will return:

```
{
        "version" : 90100,
        "protocolversion" : 70002,
        "walletversion" : 60000,
        "balance" : 7.29000000,
        "blocks" : 227166,
        "timeoffset" : 0,
        "connections" : 8,
        "proxy" : "",
        "difficulty" : 1.00000000,
        "testnet" : true,
        "keypoololdest" : 1398183964,
```

```
        "keypoolsize" : 101,
        "paytxfee" : 0.00000000,
        "errors" : ""
    }
```

where errors field is empty because there's no alert at the time I called getinfo.

Chapter 7: Keys

Private key

Private key is random 256-bit number, which can be represented in different formats, in hexadecimal format it's 32 bytes, or 64 characters in the range of 0-9 or A-F. Public key and Bitcoin address are derived from the private key, this process can't be reversed, there's no way to obtain the private key from the address or the public key. Private key is used to sign messages, and the public key can be used to verify that the signature was generated by the private key without revealing it. The mechanism of deriving public key from the private key, signing messages and verifying signature is achieved by Elliptic curve digital signature algorithm ECDSA, Bitcoin uses secp256k1 curve, we'll use Python ECDSA library to derive public key from its corresponding private key without diving into how it works, at the end of this chapter you'll find references for understanding ECDSA.

```python
# python
import os
# private key: random 256-bit number
pk = os.urandom(32)
# hex-encoded private key
pk_hex = pk.encode("hex")
```

Bitcoin Core version 0.5.0 introduced two methods for signing messages and verifying signatures, signmessage and verifymessage, both methods require unlocked wallets:

```
signmessage <address> <message>
```

<message> will be signed using the private key of <address>, will return
the signature of the message encoded in base64:

```
addr = "msQkEKvKai3ugw3HwZztkwsd34KNVCkU6J"
msg = "In cryptography we trust"
sig = bitcoin.signmessage(addr, msg)
```

will return:

H5u9INtB0HULWHT/kSFoWyhGBTYoKM8YiPnF0Q5eijWDqdPQPFlikx67msHJFzrS
bDaSEudCl8C+ucli6/HuWug=

If you tried to sign a message using foreign address -address that isn't in
your wallet, you'll get "Private key not available" error with code -4.

signmessage method will return different output every time you call it.

```
verifymessage <address> <signature> <message>
```

will return True if base64 <signature> is the result of signing <message>
using <address>'s private key, using the values from the previous example:

```
bitcoin.verifymessage(addr, sig, msg)
```

will return True.

Private key is used to spend funds received on its address by signing transaction scripts of transactions that spend those funds as we saw in Chapter 5: Transactions signrawtransaction method, anyone in the Bitcoin network can verify that you're the owner of the coins and the transaction is valid by verifying the transaction signature using your public key.

Importing Private key

You can import private key of foreign address to Bitcoin core client using importprivkey method:

```
importprivkey <WIF> [label] [rescan=True]
```

where <WIF> is the wallet import format of the private key, it's the format that's returned by dumpprivkey method, in the next section you will learn how to get this format from the hex-encoded private key, [label] is the label of the account that will be created and associated with the address of this private key, [rescan] is boolean default to True to rescan the blockchain for unspent transaction outputs associated with this private key's address. If unspent transaction outputs are found, your address's account balance and your wallet's total balance will increase. The scanning process will take sometime depending on the size of the blockchain and the speed of your computer.

```
    privkey =
"cSsQbMApJFdSAnyaAsTiYn4DFbSnLddapEpxtVj3isKzKTTq78o3"
    bitcoin.importprivkey(privkey, "foo")
```

this code will import private key starting with cSsQbMAp... , will add bitcoin address msQkEKvKai3ugw3HwZztkwsd34KNVCkU6J to my receiving addresses and associate it to "foo" account, and will rescan the block chain for unspent transaction outputs associated with this address and will update my account/wallet balance.

If you called importprivkey with invalid private key like 123456, you will get "Invalid private key encoding" error with code -5. 123456 is valid private key within 256-bit number range but isn't a valid wallet import format !

Wallet Import Format

Wallet import format is the most common way to represent private keys in Bitcoin. It's returned by dumpprivkey method which is used to obtain the private key of the given in-wallet address as we saw in <u>Chapter 4: Accounts and Addresses</u>. It's also required by importprivkey method which is used to import a foreign private key to your wallet as we saw in the previous section. Wallet import format is shorter with built in error checking codes, so typos can be detected easily which is impossible in hex format.

WIF is simply base58check encoded private key, with 0x80 version byte in case of mainnet, and 0xef in case of testnet. Base58check encoding is discussed in the next section.

Given a private key pk:

```
# python
import os
pk = os.urandom(32)
# hex-encoded private key
x = pk.encode("hex")
```

which will return this hex-encoded private key:

6a802aa43f615fb69eb56ecccf14907f3e68f139c58dbfaf436da6c7a8e921ac

Using base58checkencode function that we will implement in the next section:

```
# mainnet
wif = base58checkencode(0x80, pk)
# testnet
wif2 = base256checkencode(0xef, pk)
```

If you're on testnet and imported wif2 "92PpaZJkgETEEopiprZbRK1NGDiDGnpzGEN2fXM6pubYE2iYSXy" using importprivkey method, address n1kqMBuzNAnMjE6YVdWZXffTiuhyvPp2Kn will be added to your "Receiving addresses" and blockchain will be scanned for unspent transaction outputs related to this private key's address.

Base58check encoding/decoding

Bitcoin uses a modified base58 binary-to-text encoding to encode byte arrays into human readable strings. We will use base58check to get the wallet import format from the private key, the Bitcoin address from the public key, and to get multi-sig address from the redeemScript.

Base58check has the following features:

- Base58check accepts arbitrarily sized payload, and uses a set of 58 alphanumeric symbols consisting of easily distinguished lowercase and uppercase letters to eliminate visual ambiguity of similarly looking characters in some fonts, where capital o "O" and zero "0" are omitted, and small lowercase L "l" and uppercase i "I" are omitted.

123456789ABCDEFGHJKLMNPQRSTUVWXYZabcdefghijkmnopqrstuvwxyz

- Base58check uses one byte for version, Bitcoin address for example uses 0x00 version byte for addresses on the mainnet.

- Base58check generates a 4 bytes checksum, which can be used to automatically detect errors as we'll see in "WIF checksum checking" section.

- Base58check preserves leading zeros in the data.

So, how to create a base58check encoded string, given *version byte* and *payload* ?

1) Concatenate the version byte and the payload bytes.
2) Take the first four bytes of the double SHA256 application of step1 SHA256(SHA256(step1)), these four bytes are the checksum.
3) Concatenate the result of step1 with the four bytes checksum of step2.
4) Convert the result of step3 into a big-endian number.
5) Count the number of leading zeros in result of step3.
6) Convert the result of step4 into base58 using bignum division and base58 alphabet.
7) Concatenate "1" repeated n times (n is the result from step5) and the result of step6.

Here's a simple implementation of base58check encoding:

```python
# python
import hashlib
# base58check alphabet
```

```
        alphabet =
"123456789ABCDEFGHJKLMNPQRSTUVWXYZabcdefghijkmnopqrstuvwxyz"

    def base58checkencode(version, payload):
        s = chr(verion) + payload
        sha = hashlib.sha256
        double_sha = sha(sha(s).digest()).digest()
        checksum = double_sha[:4]
        s2 = s + checksum
        bignum = base256decode(s2)
        zeros_count = count_leading_chars(s2, "\0")
        return "1" * zeros_count + base58encode(bignum)

    def base58encode(n):
        result = ""
        while n > 0:
            result = alphabet[n%58] + result
            n /= 58
        return result

    def base256decode(s):
        result = 0
        for c in s:
            result = result * 256 + ord(c)
        return result

    def count_leading_chars(s, ch):
        count = 0
        for c in s:
            if c == ch:
                count += 0
            else:
                break
        return count
```

What if you want to get the payload and the version bytes from a base58check encoded string ? You'll need to reverse the steps of base58checkencode function. We will use this decode function in the next sections to get the private key from the WIF, and to get the public key hash from the bitcoin address. Here's a simple implementation of base58check**decode** function:

```
def base58checkdecode(s):
    ones_count = count_leading_chars(s, "\1")
    bignum = base58decode(s)
    s2 = base256encode(bignum)
    result = "\0" * ones_count + s2
    version = result[:1].encode("hex")
    payload = result[1:-4].encode("hex")
    checksum = result[-4:].encode("hex")
    return {
        "version": version,
        "payload": payload,
        "checksum": checksum
    }

def base58decode(s):
    result = 0
    for i in range(0, len(s)):
        result = result * 58 + alphabet.index(s[i])
    return result

def base256encode(n):
    result = ""
    while n > 0:
        result = chr(n % 256) + result
        n /= 256
    return result
```

WIF to private key

WIF is the base58check encoded private key, using base58check**decode** function we can get the hex-encoded private key, given a WIF:

```
wif="92PpaZJkgETEEopiprZbRK1NGDiDGnpzGEN2fXM6pubYE2iYSXy"
```

call base58checkdecode function:

```
result = base58checkdecode(wif)
```

will return:

```
{
    'checksum': '25f72c50',
    'version': 'ef',
    'payload':
'6a802aa43f615fb69eb56ecccf14907f3e68f139c58dbfaf436da6c7a8e921a
c'
}
```

where payload is our private key.

WIF Checksum Checking

Given a wallet import format:

```
wif="92PpaZJkgETEEopiprZbRK1NGDiDGnpzGEN2fXM6pubYE2iYSXy"
```

How can you tell if this wif is valid prior to importing it to your wallet ?
Using checksum embedded in the wif we can tell if it's valid or not. We will
compare the double sha256 of version+payload against checksum for
equality. If both are equal, the wif is valid.

```
result = base58checkdecode(wif)
v = result["version"].decode("hex")
p = result["payload"].decode("hex")
c = result["checksum"].decode("hex")
vp = (v + p)
assert sha(sha(vp).digest()).digest()[:4] == c
```

Compressed Private Key and WIF

Compressed private key is the uncompressed hex-encoded private key with
suffix 0x01, this means that compressed private key is one byte longer than
uncompressed private key !

```
# python
import os
# uncompressed private key
p = os.urandom(32)

# hex-encoded uncompressed private key
x = p.encode("hex")
#
3b6cea54ea6086929ebda467759b41ff517da5b25feceb52bba7fb0e80cc17c0

# hex-encoded compressed private key
c = x + "01"
#
3b6cea54ea6086929ebda467759b41ff517da5b25feceb52bba7fb0e80cc17c0
01
```

133

Why then it's called compressed ? Because it's used to generate *compressed public key*. Compressed public key is half the size of the uncompressed public key.

Uncompressed private key → uncompressed public key → Address1.

Uncompressed private key + 0x01 → compressed private key → compressed public key → Address2.

Each private key format (compressed, and uncompressed) has a corresponding WIF:

```
# testnet
wif_uncompressed = base58checkencode(0xef, p)
# 923678o8MBih62SfaT7R93WPRXPYmLsQasDxM6CJBDcTewqfxQh
wif_compressed = base58checkencode(0xef, c.decode("hex"))
# cPaDY5QbS6K1wBNHGeFKYW4hyF8XCihV6UgBHfvrp6fWdzemvHr6
```

On mainnet, WIF of uncompressed private key starts with "5", and uncompressed starts with "K". On testnet WIF of compressed private key starts with 9, and uncompressed starts with "c".

When importing WIF using importprivkey method, how Bitcoin Core client knows if this WIF is derived from compressed or uncompressed private key to scan the block chain for unspent transaction outputs related to compressed public key and its address, or related to uncompressed public key and its address ?

WIF is base58check encoded private key. Using base58check decoding to extract the private key from WIF. If the private key is compressed -ending with 0x01, scan the blockchain for outputs related to the compressed public key and its address. If the private key is uncompressed, scan the blockchain for outputs related to the uncompressed public key and its address.

Public key

Public key is 512-bit number, derived from the private key using Elliptic curve digital signature algorithm ECDA where Bitcoin uses secp256k1 curve. Uncompressed public key is a point on the elleptic curve consisting of a pair of (x,y) coordinates, and represented externally as hex-encoded 65 bytes (130 hex digits), 1 byte 0x04, 32 bytes representing x-coordinate, and 32 bytes representing y-coordinate. We'll discuss compressed public key in the next section. Public key is used to verify that a given signature was generated using its mathematically associated private key or not as we saw in verifymessage method.

You will encounter public keys in different places. For example in the output of validateaddress method, where pubKey in the returned object is the hex-encoded raw public key. You'll find it in scriptPubKey of "pay to pubkey hash" transaction output script:

```
OP_DUP OP_HASH160 <pubKeyHash> ...
```

Using Python-ECDSA library https://github.com/warner/python-ecdsa we will generate a SigningKey (private key), derive a VerifyingKey (public key) from the SigningKey, sign messages and verify signatures:

```
import ecdsa
sk = ecdsa.SigningKey.generate() # uses NIST192p curve
vk = sk.verifying_key
sig = sk.sign("message")
assert vk.verify(sig, "message")
```

to generate SigningKey from another curve, pass curve parameter to generate method:

```
# Bitcoin uses Secp256k1 curve
sk = ecdsa.SigningKey.generate(curve=ecdsa.SECP256k1)
```

to generate SigningKey from a byte string, use from_string method:

```
import os, ecdsa
# private key
pk = os.urandom(32)
# signing key
sk = ecdsa.SigningKey.from_string(pk,
curve=ecdsa.SECP256k1)
```

Finally to generate public key from private key:

```
import os, ecdsa
# private key
pk = os.urandom(32)
sk = ecdsa.SigningKey.from_string(pk,
curve=ecdsa.SECP256k1)
vk = sk.verifying_key
# hex-encoded public key
("\04" + vk.to_string()).encode("hex")
```

Compressed Public Key

Compressed public keys were introduced to bitcoin to reduce the size of transactions and the blockchain. Compressed public key is half the size of the uncompressed public key. Compressed public key is generated from compressed private key, and represented externally as hex-encoded 33 bytes (66 hex digits) of 0x02 byte + 32 bytes representing x-coordinate if y-coordinate is even, or 0x03 byte + 32 bytes representing x-coordinate if y-coordinate is odd. Uncompressed public key consists of 0x04 byte + 32 bytes representing x-coordinate + 32 bytes representing y-coordinate.

Compressed public key can be derived from uncompressed public key easy, check the 32 bytes that represent the y-coordinate in uncompressed public key. If y-coordinate is even, our compressed public key is 0x02 + x-coordinate. If y-coordinate is odd, our compressed public key is 0x03 + x-coordinate.

Here's a simple implementation of deriving compressed public:

```python
# python
import os, ecdsa

# private key
p = os.urandom(32)
# hex-encoded private key
x = p.encode("hex")
# hex-encoded (compressed) private key
xc = x + "01"
sk = ecdsa.SigningKey.from_string(p, curve=ecdsa.SECP256k1)
# public key (x,y) point
vk = sk.verifying_key.to_string()
# x-coordiate
x = vk[:32].encode("hex")
# y-coordinate
y = vk[32:].encode("hex")
# integer y-coordinate
yint = int(y, base=16)
# if y-coordinate is even
if yint % 2 == 0:
    pk = "02" + x
# if y-coordinate is odd
else:
    pk = "03" + x
print "Compressed public key", pk
```

Address

Bitcoin address is base58check encoded public key hash with network version 0x00 in case of mainnet and 0x6f in case of testnet, here's an implementation of deriving an address from private key:

```
import os, hashlib, ecdsa, base58check
# mainnet address [0x00 | public key hash | checksum]
# testnet address [0x6f | public key hash | checksum]
# private key
privKey = os.urandom(32)
sigKey = ecdsa.SigningKey.from_string(privKey,
curve=SECP256k1)
verKey = sigKey.verifying_key
# public key
pubKey = "\04" + verKey.to_string()
sha256 = hashlib.sha256
ripemd160 = hashlib.new("ripemd160")
ripemd160.update(sha256(pubKey).digest())
# public hey hash = ripemd160(sha256(public key))
pubKeyHash = ripemd160.digest()
# testnet address
addr = base58checkencode(0x6f, pubKeyHash)
```

In my case this will return testnet address mn622EqHsHR78idQ6z1RnAPa5LGucKgpRz which is perfectly valid bitcoin address, it will return another address in your case because private key is random, you can validate it using validateaddress method:

```
bitcoin-cli validateaddress
"mn622EqHsHR78idQ6z1RnAPa5LGucKgpRz"
```

will return:

```
{
        "isvalid" : true,
        "address" : "mn622EqHsHR78idQ6z1RnAPa5LGucKgpRz",
        "ismine" : false
}
```

In the previous output, "ismine" is false because I didn't import the WIF private key of this address to my wallet.

Address Checksum Validation

Using checksum embedded in the address, we can compare this checksum against the first four bytes of the double sha256 of (version+payload) for equality:

```
import hashlib, base58check
sha = hashlib.sha256
addr = "msj42CCGruhRsFrGATiUuh25dtxYtnpbTx"
result = base58checkdecode(addr)
v = result["version"]
p = result["payload"]
c = result["checksum"]
assert sha(sha(v+p).digest()).digest()[:4] == c
```

Multi-Sig Address

Multi-sig address is base58check encoded redeemScript hash, with 0x05 version byte in case of mainnet, and 0xc4 version byte in case of testnet. Remember our multi-sig address from Chapter 4: Addresses and Accounts, here's the output of createmultisig method:

```
{
    'address': '2MvDsu5o56NRqjwqbBo8a21TXXXSLgbNUzr',
    'redeemScript':
'5221033b0d395f522a4c8c7425f68667ff8c775c053bf9f0ed8561ae6c
```

```
e86d528cf79221032aa3bb6c74daa4bea37f8bf7a386fcde31c3732fddb
a66dc231335cd84b3b5ca2102aaf0e592677105435d647c5508a75d8a93
bb92c4bd530a57df23a987680baaeb53ae'
}
```

We'll decode the address using base58checkdecode method, then compare ripemd160(sha256(redeemScript)) against payload for equality:

```
import hashlib
result = base58checkdecode(address)
payload = result["payload"]
sha256 = hashlib.sha256
ripemd160 = hashlib.new("ripemd160")

ripemd160.update(sha256(redeemScript.decode("hex")).digest())
    redeemScriptHash = ripemd160.digest().encode("hex")
    assert redeemScriptHash == payload
```

Reference

A (relatively easy to understand) primer on elliptic curve cryptography

http://arstechnica.com/security/2013/10/a-relatively-easy-to-understand-primer-on-elliptic-curve-cryptography/

Elleptic Curve Digital Signature Algorithm (White Paper)

http://cs.ucsb.edu/~koc/ccs130h/notes/ecdsa-cert.pdf

Chapter 8: Wallets

Bitcoin wallet "wallet.dat" is located in the data directory which depends on your OS as we discussed before in Chapter 1: Bitcoin Server. Bitcoin 0.8 switches from Berkeley database to LevelDB from Google. Wallet encryption feature was introduced in Bitcoin 0.4. Wallet encryption uses AES-256-CBC Algorithm to encrypt your ECDSA private keys only, not the whole wallet. The key used for encryption is derived from user's <passphrase> using SHA512 and OpenSSL's EVP_BytesToKey method and a dynamic number of rounds determined by the speed of the machine which does the initial encryption, so it's completely random and unpredictable.

After you encrypt your wallet, bitcoind will shut down, and the next time it starts it will start as normal but with your ECDSA private keys encrypted. When you need to do an operation that requires your private keys or wallet passphrase as key pool refilling or sending bitcoins, bitcoind will return an error -13 indicating that the wallet need to be unlocked using walletpassphrase method as we will see in the next sections. When the wallet is unlocked, the decryption key is stored in memory and methods that require unlocked wallet won't raise any errors, and the decryption key will be removed again if you call walletlock method, or if the time specified in the second argument to walletpassphrase method is over.

Bitcoin wallet contains:

- Private and Public key pairs for each address.

- Outgoing and ingoing transaction from/to your wallet.

- User settings.

- Default keys: private keys of the default account.

- Reserve keys: private keys of the addresses that hasn't been revealed to the user yet.

- Accounts.

- Version number.

- Key pool.

- Information about the best block chain.

Selecting Wallet File

By default bitcoind or bitcoin-qt operate on wallet file called walled.dat within the data directory. If you're on mainnet, it's wallet.dat file in data directory root. If you're on testnet, it's wallet.dat file in testnet3 directory under data directory. If you're in -regtest mode, it's wallet.dat file in regtest directory under data directory.

You can change this wallet using -wallet command line argument:

```
bitcoind -wallet=mywallet.dat
```

or you can add wallet option to your bitcoin.conf file:

```
wallet=mywallet.dat
```

Encrypting Wallet

You can encrypt your wallet using encryptwallet method:

```
encryptwallet <passphrase>
```

where <passphrase> is your super secure password. After encrypting your wallet, Bitcoin server will stop, so you need to restart your Bitcoin server to run with the encrypted wallet, and the key pool will be flushed so you'll need to make a new backup.

Here's the response of a bitcoind instance running with -printtoconsole command-line argument after calling encryptwallet method:

```
ThreadRPCServer method=encryptwallet
Encrypting Wallet with an nDeriveIterations of 58743
CWallet::NewKeyPool wrote 100 new keys
Rewriting wallet.dat...
Shutdown : In progress...
addcon thread interrupt
dumpaddr thread stop
msghand thread interrupt
Flush(false)
wallet.dat refcount=0
wallet.dat checkpoint
net thread interrupt
wallet.dat detach
wallet.dat closed
DBFlush(false) ended                109ms
StopNode()
Flushed 13293 addresses to peers.dat  91ms
Committing 3576 changed transactions to coin database...
Flush(true)
wallet.dat refcount=0
wallet.dat checkpoint
wallet.dat detach
wallet.dat closed
DBFlush(true) ended                 91ms
Shutdown : done
```

If you tried to encrypt a wallet that's already encrypted, you'll get "running with an encrypted wallet, but encryptwallet was called" error with code -15.

```python
#python
try:
    bitcoin.encryptwallet("123456789")
except JSONRPCException as e:
    print e.error["message"]
    if e.error["code"] == -15:
        # wallet is already encrypted
```

Changing Wallet Passphrase

If you want to change wallet passphrase of an encrypted wallet, use walletpassphrase method:

```
walletpassphrasechange <old-passphrase> <new-passphrase>
```

which will change the wallet passphrase from <old-passphrase> to <new-passphrase>. If you entered wrong <old-passphrase>, you'll get "The wallet passphrase entered was incorrect" error with code -14. If you tried to change the passphrase of an unencrypted wallet, you'll get "running with an unencrypted wallet, but walletpassphrasechange was called" error with code -15.

```python
#python
try:
    oldpass = "0ldp0ssw0rd"
    newpass = "newp0ssw0rd"
    bitcoin.walletpassphrasechange(oldpass, newpass)
except JSONRPCException as e:
```

```
    code = e.error["code"]
    if code == -15:
        # wallet is unencrypted
    if code == -14:
        # wrong password
```

Unlocking Wallet

If you want to unlock a locked wallet, use walletpassphrase method to unlock the wallet and store the wallet decryption key in memory for <timeout> seconds:

```
walletpassphrase <passphrase> <timeout>
```

where <passphrase> is the super secure password you entered before to encrypt your wallet.

```
walletpassphrase "my super secure password" 60
```

this will unlock my wallet for 1 minute. Note that the wallet will be locked again after <timeout> seconds.

If you used walletpassphrase on an unencrypted wallet you'll get "running with an unencrypted wallet, but walletpassphrase was called" error with code -15.

If you tried to unlock *already unlocked* wallet, you'll get "Wallet is already unlocked" error with code -17. This behavior has been changed in Bitcoin 0.9.0+ so that unlocking already unlocked wallet will change the lock time to (now + <timeout> seconds) so you won't get the previous error.

```python
#python
try:
    bitcoin.walletpassphrase("my super secure password",
60)
    # again
    bitcoin.walletpassphrase("my super secure password",
60)
    # will work fine in Bitcoin 0.9
    # new lock time = now + 60 seconds
except JSONRPCException as e:
    # Up to Bitcoin 0.8 only
    if e.error["code"] == -17:
        # Wallet is already unlocked
```

Here's a list of methods that require unlocked wallet, arranged alphabetically:

1) dumpprivkey

2) getrawchangeaddress

3) importprivkey

4) keypoolrefill

5) sendfrom

6) sendmany

7) sendtoaddress

8) signmessage

9) signrawtransaction

Locking Wallet

If you want to lock an unlocked wallet, use walletlock method, which will remove wallet decryption key from memory. You will need to call walletpassphrase again before using methods that require wallet to be unlocked:

```python
# python
# unlock my wallet for 60 seconds
bitcoin.walletpassphrase("myp0ssw0rd", 60)
bitcoin.keypoolrefill()
# lock wallet again, don't wait to be locked automatically
bitcoin.walletlock()
```

Backup wallet

You need to backup your wallet so that if your current wallet is corrupted or lost, your service won't be affected. Schedule your wallet backup so that the most recent backup contains keys not used yet, so that if you restore this backup and used it, you won't lose any coins.

Use backupwallet method to backup your wallet:

```
backupwallet <destination>
```

where <destination> is a directory or a path with filename. If you give it a filename, it will safely backup your wallet to the current user directory. If you give it a directory, the directory should exist before calling backupwallet and you've the permission to write to this directory or you'll get "Wallet backup failed" error with code -4.

```python
#python
try:
        bitcoin.backupwallet("e:/walletbackups")
```

```
except JSONRPCException as e:
    if e.error["code"] == -4:
        # directory doesn't exist, or no write permission
```

Schedule your wallet backup every (n) address generation and transactions, where (n) should be less than the key pool size. For example if your key pool size is 1000, you should backup your wallet each ~ 750 address generation and transaction, and force key pool refill in case of encrypted wallet, so that your most recent backup contain keys not used yet.

In the next image the gray vertical bars are most current backup key pool and the current wallet key pool. Note that they are the same because i backed up my wallet before getting any new address from the keypool. Bar above the horizontal dotted lines represents the addresses used from the current key pool.

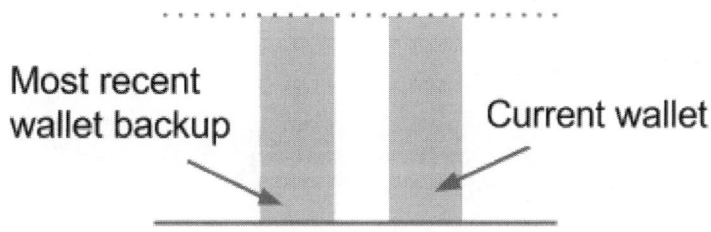

If you generated 300 new keys, 300 keys will be taken out of the key pool (above the dotted line), and 300 new keys will be generated to fill the key pool (dark grey above the solid line) in the next picture. At this point the previous backup is still valid, because the used keys are in the most recent backup, and the new keys (dark gray) are not used.

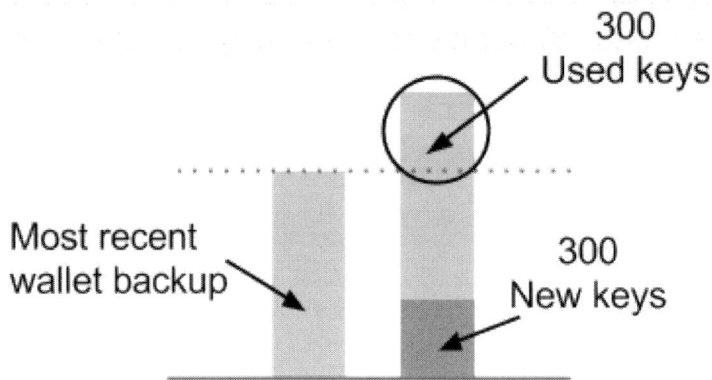

If you generated another 700 keys, 700 keys will be taken out of the key pool, and 700 new keys will be generated to fill the key pool, at this point the previous backup is still valid but you should create a new backup in order not to lose any of your coins if you lost your current wallet.

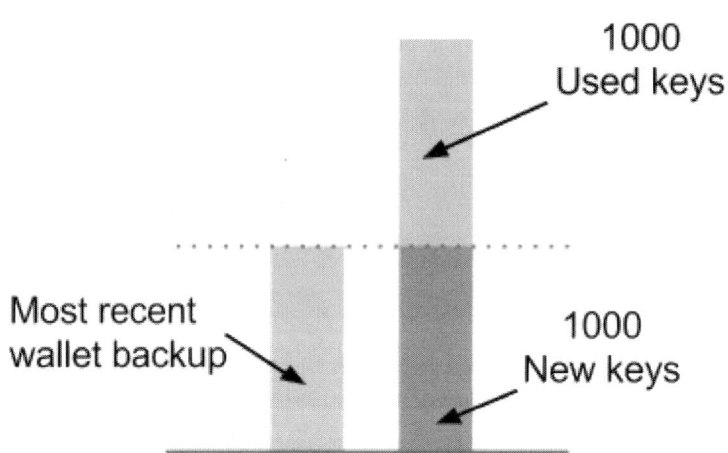

In the next picture, if you generated another 100 keys, this make the previous backup obsolete. If you lose your wallet, the 100 keys represented by the dark gray bar above the dotted line will be lost and the most recent backup won't help you, because they aren't in the most recent backup, you should have made a backup before the keys in you wallet is greater than your key pool size.

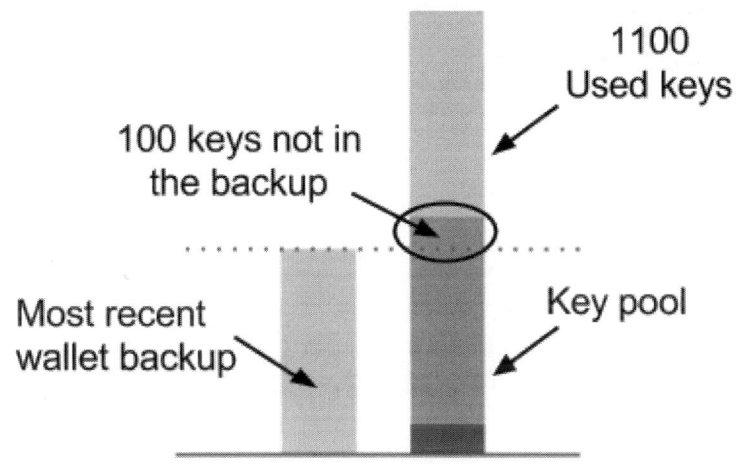

Dumping Wallet

Bitcoin Core client version 0.9.0 introduced dumpwallet method, which is used to dump all wallet keys in human-readable format:

```
dumpwallet <filename>
```

where <filename> is the filename of the dump:

```
bitcoin-cli walletdump "~/mywallet.txt"
```

Here's a picture of the contents of mywallet.txt file:

```
mywallet.txt ×

# Wallet dump created by Bitcoin v0.9.1.0-g026a939-beta (Tue, 8 Apr 2014 12:04:06 +0200)
# * Created on 2014-05-29T21:44:00Z
# * Best block at time of backup was 245910 (00000000c5059f0baf7443f56bc90d4f5113e47a27529788f2377b6d109cb684),
#   mined on 2014-05-29T22:22:27Z

cPHFH9pBAv4JdcHx6Qdxv663uRwMAUr4PMjZqSygeQzUgCV6qBgE 2014-05-21T20:42:56Z label=Foo # addr=mqwbK1tpnN2f8X6yZwW2ZSqMGKjD8fyhoy
cPJMhLsHoWSR3DXhsrXjA9zMpKtmWnmxzQG8dzoSYEekuntYXj6b 2014-05-21T20:42:56Z reserve=1 # addr=mvaj4irhy8D1Xqg8Hook3SsCG62FfRPNul
cRKbKCGqmm35XxJfPoJz4MBQJM2DAS25MU2Qi2P7ZNAEm7K6Lj5S 2014-05-21T20:42:56Z label=Bar # addr=myt9iyKQnRRRRL2foLqTepA4vZcT2Xja2S
cSHFYYc25NDxTjiksZ2NjuULKXni6DdtM8ib1QVxC73WhZxQpYpV 2014-05-21T20:42:56Z label=[] # addr=mv1VApqvuqTjJV6miqSgw4T9LtmJeU8hhk
cUveBRjjYWw6zHnSgqWqQwMimyHMDEXwc11bF8CVtqVLQdjNCAcT 2014-05-21T20:42:56Z label= # addr=n1aB4zKE2k633cnDUcmxFgj3jcv4YKnJGb
cNq6ZvRidCKLTrg2vZS7vBcNQ2pY1z9uo7mcLMDbHz4Mu9P7aftz 2014-05-21T20:42:56Z label=Foo # addr=mveBRwjGDs5nO4oofEhsb6y2W2bqmgeiSD
cUhenKa62XctcFyv3ebxRau1AMxpUFZpS52rt1mh97W67EJZN9cY 2014-05-21T20:42:56Z reserve=1 # addr=mfxyDWEtjcuEPkNXGADaick4DiWbsiTENx
cVapV7NtDSESZRv8vpPduCL6dsWzUwzmWK1smxr7j5V9zJ7jLg2M 2014-05-21T20:42:56Z label= # addr=mjnW7XYos3vMyXGZUzU1CJFMSA3dRcPNRt
cQpMruTjEqXQMYvx7ox1zgvPdaiJLgxGJk2VkMw3E28miEAAf5hH 2014-05-21T20:42:56Z change=1 # addr=mzZR1ynAaWSKL6Y8ghjeQpNNEqxDo2aTcs
cSz7TtfLMN4BUpxWZJK37WtBAEFhWnanogDzmRLNgr6M8xBpgVQP 2014-05-21T20:42:56Z reserve=1 # addr=mkSWnmTkmyT2mugS6USD5p8BCu7G16QFxb
cVi9MYtij4xvD8E4KvRRdhBanz9m5WwcRKAJetB6tXiMFeFV1a9e 2014-05-21T20:42:56Z reserve=1 # addr=mu5Z95WfbtaXQMVcxTYxwVGmUYDXMx2wNN
cVF2DLSncZmb2X2C8xF1VxBRY3sxahGiJnX1z6SUFC8ybMUhDUqp 2014-05-21T20:42:56Z reserve=1 # addr=mwprCP6qF5wPrHit1xFFBUCm7gPtbjgfux
cU2widxnjBEPSB3c9RP7AKezoGepxQdD9CKqb5u6TRdoKKz47voE 2014-05-21T20:42:56Z reserve=1 # addr=mt5RiroXSqt1aNSJG3KFMEPATaHeEM9aVz
cV7aSkQKK2Vk1wWv2FpZSXM64MLCvqBfyciCJg2P4eedZfUey22w 2014-05-21T20:42:57Z reserve=1 # addr=mtAfZUqGnQJ2jW2QzsDWqqqU9s7tYwVPoa
cTU92c5kn4CmzTXRsSH1JhtUaubxkeAFWFoNXqjbRrLNPLhNJJRw 2014-05-21T20:42:57Z reserve=1 # addr=n1PD815cFjO3SbE5PBk6CouvTUiBhKKnTL
cQdG1tyy4sfk3xM2BXcNLVPzs1ohXnGg8ntEnmr83ikAiraBPFxt 2014-05-21T20:42:57Z reserve=1 # addr=mnYoTJyLEkGs3q51LdDovRtfSgxwWWMmks
cUTf4hzL78jP2mHosSSzQVJYfZFKEXA6p37znjquRmyF9RAsdf9R 2014-05-21T20:42:57Z reserve=1 # addr=mhU5vHVcUaSqgZ98qw1mwmrJrCX5EveruU
cRhaxQ3xXzfgvuU9tGzwwD9xnutWHb5ZjoYTVpQTRsGQh2dKPxiA 2014-05-21T20:42:57Z reserve=1 # addr=miBJn5ZEzko2pxuNvQaggrDAYKKJxE2vj8
cOfjYCdd6PghUaQNX65BMV7zTMi9NtYqfaWwJpcJRnM3hUsm7p6d 2014-05-21T20:42:57Z reserve=1 # addr=muX38FDi3BdgL6NH4ZUf7zfXTdQJbcHS8n
cVmYgYA7wwdHsX2yVkUVdF7oHqPHQWqs3m5ewakgTY5c9kCTpy8t 2014-05-21T20:42:57Z reserve=1 # addr=n1Zfu42JhjF6f1Cv8Y3oLCmtABL5HNCnNZ
cNHae1Ex6U9dfPSoMUubYbQyFy6Y7fmukpyWn9B4aP4xyqoZ4GwU 2014-05-21T20:42:57Z reserve=1 # addr=mo5b9bj5CMuyN1ngrZyc8VEU7avbXjuy5X
cSZegnYsi3b66XDLorgQ4H77byjKRBZ1NYVe4z5raHbM2qkKS4nA 2014-05-21T20:42:57Z reserve=1 # addr=mkSDd2NyuxE6cB6SXVbVjj8wY7cMs9V8mp
cN6uzVHsaCrg6MTEadBUkVzDFEWN3AjN8qmcGKx5HTUFeYPMpZmX 2014-05-21T20:42:57Z reserve=1 # addr=mzTyRVzCLTzejrmn4V1sp8DwYXahJfQHiF
cTq25NYo7UyWpKTJW6uS6j2atH7E2wb5NW8gLwSj91YAsneQbWcf 2014-05-21T20:42:57Z reserve=1 # addr=mvtzMomZVyWuf7qASGHhmRKgMjNzwi2dCg
cRmvDqQbGCwztC4EF7SoTseTK5GsBKLyZ8CayeMCrBdQnuzQG2nP 2014-05-21T20:42:57Z reserve=1 # addr=n4h1gZQbNC86SViScLBom22qkAEQRSXdEV
cNkWWsh3pcg7HTRjCB9uwNauyDRkQrWzC6r13cPB3C4XbVhp2HdE 2014-05-21T20:42:57Z reserve=1 # addr=mzw2VuGoisrNZVbxxSnbVQQRfUUZkR8h2x
cTYEg3L7zaYnWFkWYAgBwbsEPkD5yVL1qucBPND4uQX8nMZBrBGr 2014-05-21T20:42:57Z reserve=1 # addr=muuisMMiVHbVi6bcZ86J9o9JLfTKM8JMkH
cTWsm9tPPJGkjcKqULAi7S9LBsxU9svHGcEU2MXP2H7PEENUTktz 2014-05-21T20:42:57Z reserve=1 # addr=mzEQbg1zL6iNNNF9PmNU2C1nYRmoU3MWAw
cNJA8cAxBp1CdKMrEr5epgm3vLGe5ZhFx7Ti73QT8eGGuuYUs3Z3 2014-05-21T20:42:57Z reserve=1 # addr=mv1SkuwXjDU3DMkRnjZjDGNKRq3AwvdDwD
```

Plain Text ▾   Tab Width: 8 ▾   Ln 1, Col 1   INS

In the previous picture, each line start with a private key, then the date it was created at, addr= indicate the address associated with this private key, label= indicate the name of the account associated with this address, change=1 indicated that this address is a change address, reserve=1 indicate that this address is still in the key pool unrevealed to the user.

Importing Wallet

Bitcoin Core client version 0.9.0 introduced importwallet method, which is used to import private keys from a wallet dump file that was generated by dumpwallet method:

```
importwallet <filename>
```

where <filename> is the name of the wallet dump file. If you give it file name that doesn't exist, it'll return "Cannot open wallet dump file" error with code -8. Here's a simple example of importing mywallet.txt file that we generated in the previous section:

```
bitcoin-cli importwallet "~/mywallet.txt"
```

Appendix A – Configuration

Bitcoin settings can be changed using command-line arguments or configuration file options. Command line argument will affect the current Bitcoin session only, on the other hand configuration file option will affect Bitcoin until this option is removed.

Configuration file is a file named bitcoin.conf contains a list of key=value pairs, one per line, with optional comments starting with # character, located in the data directory.

All command-line arguments may be specified in configuration file except datadir and conf, command-line arguments override configuration file options.

If you pass unknown command-line argument, or add unknown option to the configuration file, it won't take effect.

If configuration file contains syntax error, bitcoind won't run and will reprort "Invalid configuration file syntax" error, Bitcoin-qt won't start and will report "Runtime error".

Many of the options that take boolean can also be set to off by specifying them with a "no" prefix, for example "splash" screen can be turned of with "nosplash" option.

To get all available command-line arguments:

```
bitcoind --help
```

or read init.cpp file in Bitcore Core client source code at github.

General Options

server

Run Bitcoin as server and accept command line and JSON-RPC commands. Bitcoin Core version 0.9.0 introduced -noserver.

```
Bitcoind -server
server=1
```

daemon

Run in the background as a daemon and accept commands .

```
Bitcoind -deamon
```

datadir=<dir>

datadir is command-line argument only, won't take effect if used in the configuration file. It's used to specify the data directory.

```
bitcoind -datadir=c:/new-data-dir
datadir=~/bitcoin-data #won't take effect in bitcoin.conf
```

conf=<file>

conf is command-line argument only, won't take effect if used in the configuration file. It's used to specify the configuration file, default is "bitcoin.conf".

```
bitcoind -conf=coco.conf
```

pid=<file>

Specify pid file, default is "bitcoin.pid". pid file is a file containing the current running instance of bitcoin's process identifier, to allow other processes to look it up.

Notifications

blocknotify=<cmd>

Execute command when the best block changes, %s in <cmd> is replaced by block hash.

```
# bitcoin.conf
blocknotify=python ~/block.py %s
```

walletnotify=<cmd>

Execute command when a transaction hits your wallet, %s in <cmd> is replaced by transaction ID.

```
# bitcoin.conf
walletnotify=python ~/tx.py %s
```

alertnotify=<cmd>

Execute command when a relevant alert is received, %s in <cmd> is replaced by message.

```
# bitcoin.conf
alertnotify=python ~/alert.py %s
```

Bitcoin Network

timeout=<n>

Specify connection timeout to other nodes in milliseconds, default is 5000.

Proxy=<ip:port>

Connect through SOCKS proxy.

```
-proxy=127.0.0.1:9050
```

socks=<n>

Specify the version of SOCKS proxy to use, 4 or 5, default is 5.

```
-socks=4
socks=4 #bitcoin.conf
```

tor=<ip:port>

Use SOCKS5 proxy to reach peers through tor hidden services, default is the value of -proxy. -tor Changed to -onion in Bitcoin Core version 0.9.0.

dns

Allow DNS lockups for -addnode, -seednode, and -connect.

```
-dns=1
dns=1
```

port=<port>

Listen for connection on port, default is 8333 on mainnet, and 18333 on testnet and regtest.

```
-port=1900
port=1900
```

maxconnections=<n>

Specify the maximum number of inbound+outbound connections to peers, default is 125.

```
-maxconnections=300
maxconnections=300
```

addnode=<ip>

Add a node to connect to and attempt to keep the connection open, it will tell you about the nodes connected to <ip>, and tell these nodes that you exist so they can connect to you. You can adding multiple nodes by appending multiple addnode= lines to your bitcoin.conf file.

```
addnode=213.179.202.19
```

connect=<ip>

Connect only to the specified node(s). It won't tell nodes connected to <ip> about your existence, use connect if you want to connect to trusted nodes and stay private.

```
-connect=127.0.0.1:19000
```

```
connect=127.0.0.1:19000
```

seednode=<ip>

Connect to a node to retrieve peer addresses, and disconnect.

```
-seednode=91.121.8.25
seednode=91.121.8.25
```

externalip=<ip>

Specify your own public address, by default the client uses web service to determine its own external routable IP address.

onlynet=<net>

Only connect to nodes in the specified network <net>, possible values are IPv4, IPv6 or Tor.

```
-onlynet=IPv6
onlynet=Tor
```

listen

Accept connections from outside, default is 1 if no -proxy or -connect.

discover

Discover own IP address, default is 1 when listening and no -externalip.

bind=<addr>

Bind to given address and always listen on it. Use [host]:port notation for IPv6.

dnsseed

Find peers using DNS lookup, default is 1 unless -connect.

banscore=<n>

Threshold for disconnecting misbehaving peers, default is 100. Nodes misbehaving by more than -banscore times is banned for -bantime. Nodes with local IP are exempted.

```
Banscore=999999 #very forgiving
```

bantime=<n>

Number of seconds to keep misbehaving peers from reconnecting, default is 86400 seconds (60*60*24 = 1 day).

maxreceivebuffer=<n>

Maximum per-connection receive buffer, <n>*1000 bytes, default is 5000.

maxsendbuffer=<n>

Maximum per-connection send buffer, <n>*1000 bytes, default is 1000.

upnp

Use UPnP to map the listening port, default is 0.

Testing and Debugging

testnet

Use the test network.

regtest

Enter regression test mode, which uses a special chain in which blocks can be solved instantly. This is intended for regression testing tools and app development.

debug=<category>

Output debugging information, default is 0, and <category> is optional. If <category> is not supplied, output all debugging information. <category> can be: addrman, alert, coindb, db, lock, rand, rpc, selectcoins, mempool, or net.

logtimestamps

Prepend debug output with timestamp, default is 1.

shrinkdebugfile

Shrink debug.log file on client startup, default is 1 when no -debug.

printtoconsole

Send trace/debug information to console instead of debug.log file.

debugnet

Output extra network debugging information, deprecated in Bitcoin Core version 0.8.6, use debug=net instead.

printtodebugger

Send trace/debug info to debugger. Removed in Bitcoin Core version 0.9.0.

JSON RPC

rpcuser=<user>

Username for JSON-RPC connections.

rpcpassword=<password>

Password for JSON-RPC connections.

rpcport=<port>

Listen for JSON-RPC connections on <port>, default is 8332 in mainnet and 18332 in testnet.

rpcallowip=<ip>

Allow JSON-RPC connections from specified IP address, you can use * as a wild card character. It's not recommended to allow connection from hosts outside your trusted network because rpcpassword it transmitted over the network unencrypted.

```
rpcallowip=192.168.1.*
```

rpcwait

Wait for RPC server to start , introduced in Bitcoin Core version 0.9.0.

```
bitcoin-cli -rpcwait getinfo
bitcoind -daemon
```

getinfo will wait for bitcoind to start, then will be executed.

rpcconnect=<ip>

Send commands to node running on <ip>, default is 127.0.0.1.

rpcthreads=<n>

Set the number of threads to service RPC calls, default is 4.

rpcssl

Use OpenSSL (HTTPS) for JSON-RPC connections.

rpcsslcertificatechainfile=<file.cert>

Server certificate file, default is server.cert.

rpcsslprivatekeyfile=<file.pem>

Server private key, default is server.pem.

rpcsslciphers=<ciphers>

Acceptable ciphers, default is TLSv1+HIGH:!SSLv2:!aNULL:!eNULL:!AH:!3DES:@STRENGTH. In Bitcoin Core version 0.9.0, default -rpcsslciphers updated to include TLSv1.2.

Wallet

wallet=<file>

Select wallet file, within data directory, introduced in Bitcoin Core version 0.9.0.

```
wallet=foo.dat
```

Disablewallet

Do not load the wallet and disable wallet RPC calls. If you call RPC method that depend on wallet like getnewaddress which get new address from the wallet key pool, you'll get -32601 error with "Method not found (disabled)" message.

Zapwallettxes

rebuild the wallet's transaction information, diagnostic tool implies -rescan.

```
-zapwallettxes -rescan
```

salvagewallet

Recover private keys from a corrupted wallet.dat .

Upgradewallet

Forces wallet to upgrade to the latest format.

dbcache=<n>

Set database cache size in megabytes, default is 25 megabytes.

```
dbcache=1024
```

keypool=<n>

Set key pool size to <n>, default is 100.

Blocks

blockminsize=<n>

Set minimum block size in bytes, default is 0.

blockmaxsize=<n>

Set maximum block size in bytes, default is 250000.

blockprioritysize=<n>

Set maximum size of high-priority/low-fee transactions in bytes, default is 27000.

gen

Start mining and generating blocks, default is 0, this option is similar to setgenerate method.

```
bitcoind -gen
gen=1 #bitcoin.conf
bitcoin-cli setgenerate true
```

genproclimit

Set the processor limit for when generation is on, -1 means unlimited, default is -1.

checkblocks=<n>

How many blocks to check at startup, default is 288, 0 = all.

checklevel=<n>

How thorough the block verification is, 0-4, default is 3.

loadblock=<file>

Imports blocks from external blk000??.dat file.

Rescan

Rescan the block chain for missing wallet transactions.

reindex

Rebuild block chain index from current blk000??.dat files.

par=<n>

Set the number of script verification threads, up to 16, 0 = auto, -n = leave n cores free, default is 0 (auto).

Transactions

mintxfee=<m.n>

Minimum fee per kilobyte of transaction to include in your blocks, fees smaller than this are considered zero fee, default is 0.01 mbtc in Bitcoin Core version 0.9.0.

paytxfee=<amt>

Fee per KB to add to transactions you send, default is 0.0 btc.

minrelaytxfee

Minimum fee per kilobyte of transaction to relay to other nodes. Fees smaller than this are considered zero fee, default is the same as -mintxfee.

limitfreerelay

Size of free transactions in kilobytes per minute to relay to other nodes, default is 15 kilobytes per minute.

spendzeroconfchange

Spend unconfirmed change when sending transactions, default is 1, can be turned off by -**no**spendzerochange.

txindex

Maintain a full transaction index, default is 0. Since Bitcoin Core version 0.8.0 a full index of historical transactions is no longer maintained, instead there's a database of unspent transaction outputs, so if you tried to look up entirely spent transaction using getrawtransaction method, you'll get "No information available about transaction" error with code -5. If you want this functionality, run bitcoind once with -txindex -reindex.

```
Bitcoind -txindex -reindex
```

Bitcoin-Qt User Interface

lang=<lang>

Set language, for example "de_DE", default is system locale.

min

Start minimized.

splash

Show splash screen on startup, default is 1.

choosedatadir

Choose data directory on startup, default is 0, introduced in Bitcoin Core version 0.9.0.

Appendix B – Error Codes

Bitcoin RPC error codes are divided into four categories:

- Standard JSON-RPC 2.0 errors.
- General application defined errors.
- P2P client errors.
- Wallet errors.

Standard JSON-RPC 2.0 errors

-32600 Invalid request.

-32601 Method not found.

-32602 Invalid parameters.

-32603 Internal error.

-32700 JSON parse error.

General application defined errors

-1 std::Exception thrown in command handling.

-2 Server is in safe mode and command is not allowed in safe mode, safe mode can be triggered using -testsafemode and disabled using -disablesafemode.

-3 Type error, unexpected type was passed as parameter, i.e: integer instead of string.

-5 Invalid Bitcoin address or private key.

-7 Ran out of memory during operation.

-8 Invalid, missing or duplicate parameter.

-20 Database error.

-22 Error parsing or validating structure in raw format.

-25 Error during transaction submission.

-26 Transaction was rejected by network rules.

-27 Transaction already in the block chain -double spend.

P2P client errors

-9 Not connected to the Bitcoin network.

-10 Still downloading initial blocks.

-23 Attempting to add node that is already added.

-24 Node has not been added before.

Wallet errors

-4 Unspecified problem with wallet.

-6 Insufficient funds in wallet or account.

-11 invalid account name.

-12 keypool ran out of keys, call keypoolrefill first.

-13 Unencrypted wallet is needed, call walletpassphrase to unencrypt your wallet.

-14 The wallet passphrase entered is incorrect.

-15 Wrong wallet encryption state, i.e: encrypting an encrypted wallet.

-16 Failed to encrypt the wallet.

-17 Wallet is already unlocked.

Printed in Great Britain
by Amazon.co.uk, Ltd.,
Marston Gate.